NO FEAR, NO FORCE

A guide to handling and training unhandled
and semi-feral foals in an ethical and gentle way

I stand alone without beliefs, the only truth I know is you.
Piper (1999–2009)

NO FEAR, NO FORCE

A guide to handling and training unhandled and semi-feral foals in an ethical and gentle way

by
Sarah Weston
Recommended Associate
of the
Intelligent Horsemanship Association

TOKEN PUBLISHING LTD
Honiton, Devon
2009
In association with
Herd Productions

First published in Great Britain, 2009 by

TOKEN PUBLISHING LIMITED
In Association with Herd Productions
Orchard House, Heathpark, Honiton, Devon EX14 1YD, UK
Telephone: 01404 46972   Fax: 01404 44788
e-mail: carol@tokenpublishing.com   Website: www.tokenpublishing.com

© 2009 Token Publishing Ltd and Sarah Weston.

ISBN 10: 1870 192 893
ISBN 13: 978 1870 192 897

Printed and bound in England by J. F. Print Ltd., Sparkford.

Contents

Foreword

I FIRST met Sarah in 2002 when she started her courses with Intelligent Horsemanship. Her previous experience, natural ability and unfailing empathy meant that she passed her courses easily and became one of my team of Recommended Associates a short time later. I have the utmost trust and confidence in her work and frequently receive positive feedback from her clients. She is a great ambassador for the work and values of Intelligent Horsemanship.

From the outset, Sarah was a champion of the little guys, small and inexpensive ponies that needed her help to integrate into the world of humans. Down to earth and practical, Sarah has an exceptional ability with unhandled and semi-feral ponies and a straightforward way of teaching others to work with them in the same way. Most importantly she has an open mind and constantly strives to hone her technique and devise ways of making it easier for the pony to trust and bond with humans.

Kelly

Kelly Marks
Director of Intelligent Horsemanship Ltd.

Sarah and Kelly attempt to make a "Pushmepullyou".

ON *a personal level I feel I can vouch directly for the efficacy of the Intelligent Horsemanship approach. Having met Sarah professionally a couple of times, she offered to come and train one of our foals, to demonstrate her technique. Due to some unfortunate circumstances "Florrie" had had to go through the drifts, which included being branded, before we could get her in. She was so shy that we had to sedate her to get her into a stable. She therefore fell most definitely into the "manhandled" category by the time we all met. Sarah saw her two days later and it was a mesmerising two hours, at the end of which Florrie was accepting the head collar being put on and off and had successfully started her leading training. She has gone from strength to strength since. Thank you Sarah!*

Rebecca Hamilton-Fletcher, MRCVS

MY *wife, Sarah, is wonderful with me but she is even better with the ponies! She has a natural ability to find a way into their souls. I sometimes think she is a horse, she even shies at leaves.*

David Vatcher

I couldn't recommend anyone more than Sarah for working with nervous, unhandled or traumatised ponies and horses.

Natalie Torr
Dartmoor Pony Training Centre

Introduction

WHAT do you do when the foal you have bought or bred won't allow you to approach him, to touch him or to go anywhere near him with a headcollar? Whether unhandled or manhandled, through nature or nurture, some foals *are* just very shy and nervous. His mother, God and instinct have all told him to avoid the predators. Predators chase, trap, restrain and kill and he knows that he should not get his head caught up, his feet caught up or enter small wooden boxes where there is no way out.

Providing a gentle, straightforward and quick technique for training your foal to accept touch and his first headcollar without fear or force, this book goes on to show how he can be taught to lead and to pick his feet up without a fight. The techniques shown are based on a true understanding of the psychology of horses and people's desire for a harmonious partnership with their horse from the outset.

Sarah Weston is a Recommended Associate of Intelligent Horsemanship Ltd and the holder of the Monty Robert's Preliminary Certificate in Horsemanship. Originally a barrister, she exchanged sober dress for sturdy boots so that she could work with horses full time. As part of her training she undertook the nattily titled project "The Psychological Implications of the Management of the New Forest Pony"otherwise known as "I'm not a picnic-nicker, I'm a picnic-nicker's mate" and she traipsed around the Forest behind commoners, agisters, verderers and the ponies themselves. Having seen examples of the best type of horsemanship and the worst, she concluded that the very best traditions are those that change with the times. Since then she has worked with every breed of semi-feral native pony foal in this country (as well as domesticated foals that are wary of being touched) and offers free foal handling to owners who are prepared to let her students work with their ponies.

Harriet and Henrietta: Dartmoor Pony Training Centre.

How the book evolved

THIS book evolved from the rough notes that I put together to send to clients that I was helping with their unhandled and manhandled foals. In time I ended up sending them all over the country and abroad to people that I couldn't reach or weren't close enough to any of the other Recommended Associates. Desperate to make a difference to the lives of the "cheap and cheerful" ponies that find their way to local markets, I would e-mail them to people and try to help them by remote control. When every one of them succeeded, I knew that I didn't have to put in a personal appearance for the methods to work; they were simple, gentle and logical and therefore relatively easy to put into practice.

Before I started writing I checked other foal books to make sure that this subject hadn't been covered. In one after the other, foals appeared almost miraculously with headcollars on. I kept asking myself, "how did that get there?!" and the more I read, the more I realised that there is a huge gap in knowledge and that all but the quietest foals probably have their first headcollars forced on them to a greater or lesser degree. Furthermore, most of them were taught to lead by force too. As the manner in which the first headcollar is introduced can have a dramatic influence on how the foal views humans in the long term, I couldn't wait to get the book published.

The technique itself is derived from the method I was shown for Handling the Untouched Horse as taught by Kelly Marks at her courses held in Oxfordshire where we have access to completely untouched horses of all shapes and sizes. These horses teach you valuable lessons about the kick zone and the essential difference between horses that have never been touched and those that have been badly touched. I was keen to develop this technique for use on semi-feral foals in the New Forest, Exmoor and Dartmoor and to avoid ropes and restraint wherever I could—armed only with a hand on a stick, a feather duster and a touch that you would use on your best boyfriend, girlfriend or teddy bear.

I was told that the Exmoor foals would be the biggest challenge of them all—these ponies don't fraternise with the tourists, have not been crossed with any other breed of horse and are arguably the wildest when they come in off the moor.

Having worked with a couple of older Exmoor ponies, I was given the opportunity to work with a set of five unhandled foals at the Exmoor Pony Centre based in Dulverton. In essence an experiment, the ponies all came round brilliantly over a long weekend and inspired us to run a course the following autumn. The ponies, Fisher, German Byte, Finisterre, Cromarty, and Portland Bill, were described by their subsequent fosterers as the tamest they had ever had. Over the next two years we worked for a fortnight at a time with a total of 70 students some of whom had never touched a pony before and over 40 raw foals mainly from the Anchor Herd. Participants described it as one of the most emotional experiences that they had ever had and one of the "Ten Things to Do Before You Die"; the foals just munched their hay and kept coming back for more.

The technique is not rocket science, it's not complicated and you don't have to be gifted to do it. You don't have to be half Gypsy, to come from generations of horsey folk or to be a horse whisperer although it helps if you can keep your voice low as well as your body language. Whilst time and patience have always helped, it is time, patience and technique that really work.

Throughout the book I refer to foals as unhandled when they could be unhandled, manhandled or really badly handled.

Graduates at the Exmoor Pony Centre.

CHAPTER ONE
Four basic concepts

Explaining the four key concepts of predator and prey; memories as pictures; pressure and release; and the "into-pressure" response.

There are four very basic but critical concepts underlying the techniques I use. The first is **PREDATOR AND PREY.** It's obvious when you think about it, that horses are prey animals and designed to run first and think later. In that way, they can avoid getting eaten. They have long, thin legs and their eyes are placed high up on their heads so that they can continue to have good all-round vision even when their heads are down to eat. Every foal whether domesticated or not, is born with the prey response as its default position. On the other hand, humans are predators—as far as horses are concerned our eyes are far too close together and our hands look uncannily like claws. Deliberately or inadvertently, we tend to act like predators too. We are very focused on what we are doing, tend to go to places in straight lines and can be quite unconscious of our body language. Horses are *never* unconscious of body language, things moving on the horizon or anything that has changed; that's their job. Their experience of humans may well mirror the actions of the lions and dogs of Africa—chase, trap, restrain, kill even when our intention is to chase, trap, restrain, cuddle! To horses, especially semi-feral ponies, eye contact is extremely important and they have to know when eye contact is significant. The direction and intensity of eye contact reveals the intent of the predator.

If in doubt, run!

I liken this prey response to transactional analysis in humans. Transactional analysis was developed in the 1950s to describe the natural inclination to react like a child if someone speaks to us like a parent—if your spouse talks down to you in this way, you have the urge to throw a tantrum or burst into tears. If your spouse talks to you as if they are a child, it's easy to become patronising and talk back like a parent. Humans however, are capable of rationalising, and by responding as an adult, they can avoid this script and bring a conversation back onto an even keel. Horses cannot rationalise in the same way and when someone acts like a predator around a horse, they have no choice but to act like a prey animal—whether by running away, defending themselves or even going somewhere else in their mind in order to cope. It's the responsibility of the human to think about the way they act, to act like a herd leader or a partner in relation to their horse and to avoid behaving like a predator (refer to page 6).

The predator/prey link goes further than this. There is a risk that when foals are subjected to what they perceive is a predatorial event, it could leave an indelible mark in their memory. After all, they have no way of knowing that the event is not life threatening or that the human may have some good reason and kind intent for what they are doing. To them, every experience is very real.

Predator	Partner	Prey
Takes a direct course from A to B	Matching behaviour	Meanders from A to B
Narrow focus	Co-operation	Wide focus
Unaware of own body language	Empathy	Extremely aware of body language / eye contact
Vocal	Leadership	Quiet
Attack the most vulnerable		Hide injury
Attack when challenged		Run when afraid
Eyes very close together		Eyes on side of head (near 360 degree vision)
Direct eye contact		Use power to run away
Use power to attack		

Transactional Analysis for Horses and Humans

Humans:

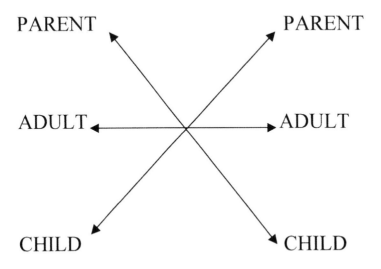

Humans with horses:

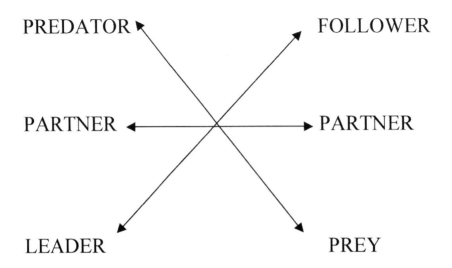

MEMORIES AS PICTURES: Horses cannot store their memories in words and yet they have extremely good memories. I surmise therefore that they can only store their memories as pictures. Our job when working with horses is to create as many pleasant pictures as we can within their "photograph album" and to replace as far as it is possible, any bad pictures that they have. When we approach a horse in a given set of circumstances, they rifle through their photograph album to find the picture that most closely resembles those circumstances in order to decide how they should feel about it; the more good pictures that they have, the more likely they are to fall upon a pleasant picture although we may have to accept that they might sometimes fall on a poor one. By using gentle systematic desensitisation; repeating and consolidating pleasant experiences, we can create more and more good pictures.

The concept of **PRESSURE AND RELEASE** is fundamental in training all horses and works particularly well with unhandled and manhandled foals. Horses establish their herd hierarchy by moving each other around. The horse that can move all the others is the herd leader and those further down the line will only be able to move those horses that are lower in the hierarchy than themselves. This movement is achieved through pressure and release. The more dominant horse uses body language—physical or mental pressure—to ask or tell the other horse to move. When the other horse has done as asked or told, the more dominant horse releases that pressure. Many of the horse's other experiences are based on pressure and release too, for example if he is attacked by a predator. The horse learns both from the pressure and the release but it is the release that seems to teach him the most. When working with a foal, we can use gentle pressure and release to communicate with him.

The into-pressure response—you pull, I pull.

The **INTO-PRESSURE RESPONSE** has been highlighted by Monty Roberts. He noticed that when a horse is pulled, his instinctive reaction is to pull back, and when a horse is pushed, his instinctive reaction is to push back. This response is designed to get horses out of trouble when faced with the perils of natural life; when predators get very close to prey animals and fleeing is not an option, they have to be able to pull away with all their strength from tearing teeth or fall into and crush predators biting at their haunches; their lives may depend on it. Many horse owners are totally unaware of this. When we put a leg against their side, we expect them to move away from the pressure. When we pull them with a lead rein, we expect them to follow us without resistance. This goes against everything they were told by their mother, God and instinct. Amazingly, horses can learn extremely quickly that they must give to a pressure and do the opposite to their natural inclination. However, unhandled and manhandled foals have not yet learned to give to pressure and still react as they would in the wild. This has important implications when tying a foal up, asking him to lead or picking up his feet for the first time. By understanding their natural response we can find ways to make it easy for them to learn to do the opposite without engaging in a fight.

You can make sure that your intervention in a foal's life is non-predatorial and go some way to negate the effects of any earlier predatorial experiences. As a foal's first owner, you can ensure that they never encounter predatorial experiences; as a second or subsequent owner you can prove to them that they have fallen on their feet and will meet logical and consistent handling.

One careful lady owner.

CHAPTER TWO
Making Faces—Reading Your Foal

How to read your foal's body language.

FOALS are very transparent about the way that they are feeling if you know what you are looking for. Once you get used to reading the signals you may be able to influence the way your foal feels, and you can even encourage him to find a way to relax. Sometimes it is mind over matter and sometimes it is matter over mind.

The easiest place to start is at his head. In all tense or nervous foals, everything braces from their ears to their lower lip. The ears may be back, the eyes unblinking and the lower lid of the eye may even twitch as if someone is pulling it down ever so slightly. The biggest give away of all is the tightened lower lip which gives the foal an undershot appearance. Add to all of this a high respiration rate, braced neck and a clamped down tail and you have got a very worried foal. Signs that are often missed are a crooked elbow or a cocked back leg (usually on the side on which you are standing) which is often confused with a resting foot; this is actually a running foot and a clear sign that the foal is reserving its right to run. It's hard to tell the difference between a running foot and a resting foot but if in doubt, it *is* a running foot.

Classic tense lower jaw.

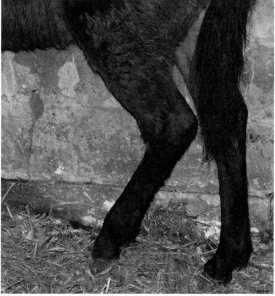

Tell-tale running foot.

By working with very low pressure as described later in this book, and very obvious releases and rewards, even with the wildest or most traumatised foal, this initial worry diminishes rapidly and starts to transform into a relaxed, relieved and confident demeanour. The ears start to move, the eye may blink and soften, the respiration rate slows down and the bottom lip relaxes. If you really use the right touch, you'll find that the top lip starts to extend and to wiggle in ecstasy as the foal realises that actually, humans can be useful. His tail will start to hang loosely too and move when it needs to. The running foot may transfer to the opposite side or disappear altogether and when he is happy with your hands on him, you can cheat a little and gently push his weight back onto that foot so that he feels more confident. Indeed with good timing, you can start to reward the demeanour that you like to see by moving away or clicking and treating to say "Thank-you, that's just what I wanted". It's a useful technique which can then follow your foal all the way through his education.

The clearest signs of relaxation are when the foal licks and chews as if digesting information, or yawns to let out energy. When he yawns, it's a perfect time to stop the session on a good note and allow him to stay in that relaxed state. It's also an indication that he may be starting to get tired[1].

Aggressive behaviour, which can be already established or brought about by a perceived need to defend himself, is even more obvious and generally happens very quickly. Biting is usually preceded by the ears being pinned back, and the teeth showing, but a kick can arrive without warning and be delivered at lightning speed. By following the route shown in this book, you can minimise the risk of being kicked by having the right equipment at the right time, in the right place and then showing the foal that there is nothing to be afraid of.

Yawning—a good sign of relaxation.

---

[1] *Excessive yawning can also be a sign of pain in horses. As with all body language, you need to be looking out for anything unusual that would indicate that something is not quite right.*

The Story of Wellow Leaf—the Golden Pony with a Golden Attitude

WELLOW Leaf, known as Baby, was owned by a local commoner who asked me to halter train him for her. I worked with two students, Lucy and Lesley, and he was happily being touched, having his headcollar on and starting to lead within an hour and half without any of the work being high pressured. When he was sold, to Linda, who had been on one of my other courses, she asked me to help with his loading. Baby settled easily in his new home and was turned out from the outset. I receive regular updates about him and was pleased to hear that all our foot handling work had paid off and he was a good boy for the farrier.

CHAPTER THREE
Using body language

Why we use body language in training foals.

I IMAGINE that the body language that we use with horses sounds like Pidgin English to them, but even the crudest body language saves the horse the trouble of translating what we mean. It's much more logical to them and in an emergency it is much more likely to get the message across. Foals, especially semi-feral foals, are completely tuned in to body language and communicate in Equus[2] from the word go. When they meet someone who is conscious and careful about their body language, the approach they take, the signals they employ and the messages they are giving—then the foals often start to relax immediately. Too often, we are completely unaware of our body language and it must be very difficult for foals to interpret what we mean.

Horses are also extremely sensitive to intent. Some people believe that horses can read our thoughts but, even if they can't, it is likely that they are so adept at reading body language that they can read the slightest tension or focus in the way that we move.

With untouched foals, the more subtle you can be with your body language, the easier it is to train them but beware that there is as much danger with a creeping predator as there is with a pouncing one. Once the foal is confident you may even find that you have to use some pretty unsubtle body language to say, "actually, that's not acceptable to me"—it helps not to be too reserved in this situation. Making "chicken wings" with your arms, slapping your coat, or even jumping up and down has a much better effect than shouting.

[2] *Monty Roberts has been hugely influential in developing the concept of the language of Equus and how it might be utilised by humans to enhance their communication with horses.*

A Bright Star—The story of Bryn

DIANA, who probably already had enough horses, spotted Bryn when she was out riding on Exmoor whilst on holiday. He stood out from all of the other Exmoor foals because he had a huge star in the middle of his forehead. If Diana hadn't bought him on the spot, his future would have been very uncertain—Exmoor foals are not allowed any white hairs in their coats. Bryn arrived at Diana's in Horsham with a headcollar already on. He didn't want her anywhere near him and the headcollar was starting to mark his face. She rang me to see whether I could help. During the first session, the priority was to befriend him and to get the tight headcollar off before it had a chance to become embedded in his flesh. The touch and move away technique worked well and once he was happy to be touched it was just a matter of getting the headcollar undone. Working with just one hand, I slowly eased the buckle undone which was difficult because it had become stiff with mud.

Once the headcollar was off, Bryn was none too keen to have a new one on. I decided to show Diana how to clicker train him so that she could offer him some really positive reward for allowing her to touch him with her hand, and then with the headcollar. Bryn picked this up really quickly and was soon happy to have his headcollar on in the stable. Understandably, the first time she turned him out, Diana was very worried that he would never be caught again. During the day she approached him in the field at regular intervals and gave him a click and a treat for being touched. When evening came, Bryn came up to be caught very easily.

CHAPTER FOUR
From Moor to Door

Explaining the typical experience of a semi-feral foal from the drift or gathering through to the sales yard.

THERE is nothing like the excitement of buying a wild foal at the sales or a posh foal from a breeder with the intention of loving and befriending it and watching it grow, physically and emotionally, and dreaming of it becoming your best friend and a show ring star. And then, there is nothing like the disappointment of realising you have bitten off more than you can chew and that your ungrateful pony will not come near you and refuses to have a head collar on despite your undying love and vast quantities of food.

When buying a semi-feral foal it is important to know what he may have already experienced in his life, so that you can have a good idea of what you may be up against when you want to train him; his experiences should not make your task impossible but may make it harder. It will mean that you have to really earn the foal's trust before you can make good progress. I have found time and time again that although it is much easier to train the unhandled foal than the manhandled foal, both can be extremely rewarding.

Knowing what may have happened to a foal in its past helps you to see life from his point of view and to work in a methodical way to erase or at least dilute any negative memories of humans that he may have.

New Forest ponies in the shade on Woodgreen Common.

Free to socialise.

Before he is taken off the forest, hill or moor, the semi-feral foal has an almost idyllic life—save for having to endure the inevitable insects, he has had every thing he needs and nothing that he doesn't—a good and tenacious mother, a protective herd, plenty of exercise, fresh air and water, lots to look at and others to play with. He has learned to be an all-terrain, all-weather pony and how to look after himself. Despite being owned he has been almost totally wild having had little if any human interaction until the day he was caught. His natural survival instinct will have been activated the day he was born and ensured that he could recognise potential threats and predators.

As well as these pleasant experiences it is important to know what may happen to some ponies running out on places such as Exmoor, Dartmoor, the Cumbrian Fells, the New Forest and the Welsh Hills once they are brought in. To most commoners and farmers, ponies and foals are just stock like any other farm animal and practicalities have to come first. Nevertheless, there is a great deal of pride in the breeding of the ponies and the tradition of commoning and farming.

Shaking off the midges!

"DRIFT" OR "GATHERING"

Typically, semi-feral foals are rounded up by commoners, agisters or farmers on horseback, and in some areas quad bikes, in what is knows as a "drift" or "gathering". These can range from a quiet drive into an enclosed area to a noisy full-blown chase at high speed. The experienced mares may have been through many times and they often know where to go; for the foals it is often their first close encounter with humans.

Between the annual drifts or gatherings, individual foals or small groups may be rounded up in what is known in some areas as colt-hunting. In some cases a foal may be brought down by someone catching hold of his tail and pulling him off balance, then jumping off their own horse on top of him. Others may be caught with ropes.

The pens or corrals used to contain the ponies are usually purpose built, but are sometimes made of makeshift materials such as low hurdles which can increase the risk of ponies getting injured if they try to escape. Ponies may be guided by body language or people using sticks or hands to move them around. A number of procedures may be carried out here including hot branding, tail marking of older horses, worming and inspections. In some cases foals will be kept with their mothers while this takes place but in others the foal will be separated from his mother. In the New Forest for example, foals tend to be kept with the mare when they are hot branded. In most cases it is a single, small brand which is applied once for a period of less than three seconds whilst two men restrain the foal against a fence. Sometimes, the commoners will twist the ear or tail of the foal in order to restrain and subdue it. The theory is that this will release endorphins which will help to negate the discomfort the foal feels when the brand is applied. In other areas foals may be separated from their mothers immediately and forcibly restrained by a rope halter fastened to something solid such as a fence whilst they are branded and inspected.

New Forest ponies coming in at Turf Hill Drift.

A well executed brand — the hair has been clipped and the foal-sized brand applied for the optimum time.

Three seconds on and then straight off…..

Exmoor foals are branded three times—once with their herd number, once with their individual number and once with the Exmoor Pony Society diamond which denotes that they are eligible for registration in the Exmoor Pony Society's Stud Book. In 2009, the Government will make it compulsory for all foals to be micro-chipped and it may be that the justification for branding as a means of identification will be lost but only if the microchips can be read from a distance and readers are readily available. However, many commoners, farmers and breed societies are protective of their brand and see it as part of their heritage. At present it is compulsory for all depastured New Forest ponies to be branded but not if they are sold as foals.

Branding executed well, does not actually seem to cause the foals to react very much at the time of application. Indeed, tamed foals don't seem to react to it at all. This gives some credence to the argument that it isn't the branding that causes the trauma but the level of handling that is required to carry it out coupled with the degree of wildness of the foal. The British Equine Veterinary Association came to the view that hot branding was preferable to freeze-branding for unhandled semi-feral ponies because less overall contact was required. Poor branding, for example where the branding iron is not heated up to the optimum temperature, may result in the branded area becoming infected especially if the brand has to be re-applied. There is no way of measuring how much pain results from a brand but it is likely to be more than the temporary pain caused by micro-chipping. Nevertheless, micro-chipping semi-feral foals will not be straightforward or pain-free as they will still have to be restrained or contained, and the needle required to insert the microchip into the nuchal ligament is a large one.

On Dartmoor and the Cumbrian Fells ear tagging and ear marking are also used as a form of identification. Ear marking involves cutting a shape into the foal's ear. It should be clear whether this has been done to your foal although tags are sometimes torn out if the foal catches it on something. On Dartmoor this may be in addition to a large brand but tends only to be used on foals that are intended to be kept out on the moor.

On Exmoor, the foals are thoroughly inspected whilst they are tied up in order to establish their eligibility for registration. This involves a close inspection of their hair all over to ensure that there are not too many white hairs and also entails picking up each one of the foal's feet.

Where halters are used at drifts and gatherings, they are made from coarse rope which tightens and continues to tighten around the nose and the head if the pony pulls back. It is almost inevitable that a semi-feral or untrained foal will pull back and keep pulling back with all of his strength.

Foals may be wormed at the round ups with oral syringes or injection usually whilst confined in a crush or chute.

In many cases, foals are abruptly weaned at the drifts and gatherings, although some commoners will bring their mares and foals in for the winter and wean at a later stage. Ponies taken off the forest or moor are loaded into stock trailers or cattle trucks and encouraged forward with sticks and the voice. Given that the foals are born throughout April, May and June, and that the earliest round ups take place in August, foals may be very young at weaning. Sometimes groups of foals are kept together when they are weaned and may be turned out. Others are kept isolated and inside for some time. This can represent a very sudden change of environment and diet. Horse behaviour experts point to this early weaning, change of diet and isolation as a trigger factor for problems such as crib-biting and weaving and the onset of gastric ulcers.

HALTER BREAKING

The most traditional way of halter breaking semi-feral foals and indeed some domesticated foals is to forcibly restrain them to put the halter on. A crush is used to restrain them or they may be held by one or more people while the halter is put on. In some cases they may then be tied up to something solid to teach them to "respect" the halter. This practise is commonly known as "swinging" or "tying on". In some cases an enclosed area is used so that they cannot pull back very far. It is argued that ponies that have been "swung" or "tied on" never learn to pull away when tied up and will always come forward when pulled. It is claimed that it is not harmful; however it is unlikely that anyone will ever check whether a pony has been harmed by this procedure as these generally cheap and cheerful ponies are less likely to receive the attention of a vet, physiotherapist

The tradition of "tying on"

or McTimoney-Corley practitioner to check this[3]. Certainly there may be no obvious visible harm and yet I often come across formerly semi-feral ponies that are chronically sore in the neck and poll.

THE SALES

Many foals are sold through sales yards local to the area in which they were caught. Some premises such a Beaulieu Road Sales Yard are purpose built from materials sympathetic to the environment and designed to make it easy and safer to move ponies around. Others are simply cattle market premises. Most are monitored carefully by welfare organisations such as World Horse Welfare and the RSPCA who have powers to intervene where animals are in particularly poor condition. However, there are still sales yards where not even small quantities of food and water are routinely provided, pens are over-crowded and ponies of mixed age, sex and origin are put in together. Sometimes the foals bite and kick each other and are unable to move away from people standing around the pens. Foals may be weaned on the day that they go to the sales and may be at the sales yard from 7 a.m. to 7 p.m. having already travelled for some time. Some find themselves being transported to one sale after another within days.

In the sales ring, it is the flashiest, high energy foals that tend to sell for the most money rather than those that are quiet and calm. The foals tend to be moved around energetically by staff albeit that sticks have now been replaced by flags.

At some sales yards written advice may be available to potential purchasers about how to handle their foal. It tends to be fairly succinct, and consists of telling them to keep the foal in for a few days on its own, to keep the headcollar on at all times, and to have a tag (small length of lead rein) attached to the headcollar permanently to make it easier to take hold of it. It is claimed that the tag will teach the foal not to fight the headcollar as the foal will tend to stand on it occasionally.

[3]*The views of a vet and a McTimoney-Corley practitioner are included at the end of this book.*

Ponies at the sales.

The inevitable disputes.

TOURIST INFORMATION

It always helps to realise what tourists may have taught the semi-feral pony. On Exmoor the ponies rarely if ever come into contact with tourists, but on Dartmoor and in the New Forest, for example, some ponies have regular contact with them. For some this may have turned them into friendly people-loving creatures that know that by just standing and looking pretty they may be given a treat. Others have learned that mugging works, and that using or threatening to use your teeth or feet results in food being dropped or thrown down as the donor retreats. Foals that have received this positive reinforcement of their dominant behaviour can be aggressive.

In the case of domesticated foals, their experiences may range from robust handling, no handling or to some really good positive handling. Some studs also tie their foals to something solid to teach them not to fight with the headcollar. It's important to be aware though that domesticated, stud bred or home bred does not necessarily mean tame. It may mean anything from over confident and pushy (where a foal has been over-petted) to very wary.

Nice car Mr!

IN THEIR NEW HOME

Many of the calls I receive relate to foals that have been turned out in a large field either straight away or after a few days and are then impossible to catch again especially if they are turned out with other similar ponies.

It is tempting with any nervous foal to turn him out to see if he will "come round" in his own good time and indeed many do. Others prove to be difficult to catch and are spooky or nervous for years. This can seem like the gentlest way to train a foal and yet logically, it cannot actually teach him how to be touched or to have a headcollar on—if it does work, it is the unlikely triumph of hope over adversity. Food may provide a great incentive to have contact with humans but ponies will not give up their safety for food or are impossible to train with clicker training because they view all hand treats as potential poison. People may spend hours sitting with their foals in fields and stables, being honoured with the occasional contact and interaction but never achieve their objectives. Indeed they may be teaching the opposite of what they think they are—if the foal learns that it can take food and just leave when it wants to, *that's* what it has actually learned. As time goes by, the foal rapidly becoming a bigger, stronger pony, becomes really adept at avoiding unwanted contact—from running away to turning its bottom rather purposefully—and whenever you are with your pony *you are* teaching it. Vast quantities of time and patience are one thing, but what if there is an emergency in the meantime? If urgent veterinary treatment, most obviously gelding, or hoof care is needed while the foal is still wild or nervous, it is likely that this will have to be met with more robust handling, reinforcing everything that the foal suspects about humans. The use of time, patience AND technique is more likely to succeed.

There is always a temptation to try and make up for anything horrid that has ever happened to your foal before he came to you. Foals that are seen as rescues are often over-petted and over-fed and allowed to dominate their owners. As well as desensitising your foal and teaching him that humans can be trusted, the most practical help you can give your foal is to be a reliable leader with some consistent ground rules—then he will learn that he can afford to relax. Horses really value clear and fair leadership.

If you are the first human that your foal has ever met then you have the luxury of choosing how he should be handled from the outset, even if your foal is semi-feral. My own mares are pretty friendly without being a nuisance to tourists and I can catch them whenever I want them. I bring them in to avoid the Drifts, and when they come home of their own accord, I feed them so that hopefully they would come back to me if they were in trouble. I don't handle the foals very much until they are weaned but I do befriend them and will, for example, pick up their feet while they are loose. I use the same techniques as I describe in this book to teach them to be touched, to have their first headcollar on, to lead and to pick their feet up.

Bringing my girls home.

Biting off more than you can chew: True stories

The scenarios described below are typical of those that appear in my e-mail inbox and on the Intelligent Horsemanship Discussion Group ...

In November I bought a 7 month old Welsh Cob colt at one of the big Welsh autumn sales. He was haltered, tied up in the pen and led in the ring; he'd also had his jaw trimmed and white socks chalked. Poor wee chap was obviously petrified by the whole huge noisy event, never having previously been off the farm. I think the handling he had before the sale has been pretty disastrous; it's convinced him that ropes are bad news, as are one or more people in a confined space with him—so in effect he's in a far worse state than if he were totally unhandled.

I have been asked to trim the feet of a 7 month old New Forest pony. He arrived at his new owners in a lorry and "fell" down the ramp at the other end. He was herded (chased!) into a 12' stable. Now nobody can get near him (I wonder why!) and stands at the back of the stable, bum to the door, ears flat back on his neck. How do you break the ice with this one? Any suggestions gratefully received.

Have got the yearling NF that I told you about. She has a head collar on but at the moment although it is only a small area she is in she is not letting me near her to catch her and she badly needs to be taught to pick her feet up and see the farrier as her toes are very long. She is also being bothered a lot by the flies so need to get some summer fly in her ears and some repellant on her.

I hope you don't mind me e-mailing you but I have recently purchased an unhandled NF colt. He is currently stabled and I have made no attempt to get a headcollar on as he doesn't like me getting too near so I haven't really tried, just talk to him and spent time in the stable with him. I obviously need to get him used to being handled soon and I also need to get him gelded at some point. As he has been stabled since Sunday I wondered if you had time to fit me in for some sessions with you.

I bought two May NF foals in November sales. As they were being loaded a lady helping said the sire of the smaller one threw foals with dodgy temperaments.
When they arrived, the transport provider insisted on putting headcollars on the foals so I could worm them and this may have been traumatic for them. Apart from that, there was nothing to upset them too much. I am still unable to touch the shier one of the two. When I wasn't thinking what I was doing, and got in the way of him and his food, he started to show threatening behaviour, gesturing as if to lunge at me. He did it a couple of times, dancing fast on his feet, spinning his back end to me and snapping his teeth at me. He is fine though now in as much as I can walk past him as long as I make no eye contact and he knows I am just going about my business.

CHAPTER FIVE
Safety, equipment and facilities

Highlighting the importance of keeping you and your foal safe from the outset, through the equipment that you use to the training environment.

ASK someone who avoids horses at all costs why he doesn't like them, and he will say "because one end bites and the other end kicks". I have also met ponies that are prepared to squash, trap, or run you over! It is natural for a pony in a confined situation to exercise these powers if it feels that it is under too much pressure. It may also hurt you entirely by accident if it is frightened or confused.

Years ago, when I started out, I worked with an unhandled New Forest colt in his owner's stable. She told me that she thought he might jump out of the stable and she provided me with a mesh panel to go in front of the door. My husband David was filming me through the mesh with a little video camera when the pony decided to go for the light and jumped straight through the mesh panel. Fortunately he was fine but David had a black eye where the video camera hit him and a mesh imprint on his shoulder—luckily the pony didn't actually land on him. The pony was unharmed but the video camera was a write off.

By using the right equipment, the right environment and the right techniques, you can minimise the likelihood of the foal leaving or resorting to self defence and the risk of you or him being injured. Nevertheless you should never work alone and always have your mobile phone available for emergencies.

It helps to think like a Health and Safety Officer—not by filling yourself with dread about what could go wrong—but by applying common sense and horse sense to the situation and carrying out a proper assessment of the risks. There is a difference between training your foal quickly and taking short cuts—the first can be achieved with the right technique providing a dramatic result in a non-dramatic way; the second might work and might not.

You need to wear a riding hat to the latest standard, sturdy boots and a body protector whenever you work with even the tiniest of foals. This will help you to feel more confident as well as making you safer. While you are thinking about clothing, choose dark colours and quiet clothes that won't make a "shushy" noise if they come into contact with the foal's body. Until I am at the leading stage, I prefer to work without gloves so that I can achieve a real contact with the foal's body, but gloves are a must once you are asking the foal to move. I prefer to wear a fleece that I have worn around horses for a few days before and not to wear any strong perfume.

The equipment I use to train an unhandled foal is inexpensive and easy to find or make. The hand on a stick is made from a glove stuffed with sponge and then firmly taped onto a stick of about 2 metres in length. The stick needs to be light but sturdy. Feather dusters can be found in most hardware shops and I find the synthetic ones are better than those made with real feathers as they do not break or moult so easily. I like to use a feather duster because they are warm, furry and a little bit bendy and it will smell of the horses you have touched before.

Home-made hand on a stick.

The headcollar needs to be made of soft webbing and most importantly to have a buckle OVER the nose and the crown piece. Make sure the buckles are easy to use and not stiff. I dislike foal slips and find that Shetland sized headcollars fit most native pony foals[4] . Leather is better still providing it is really soft and pliable. The headcollar should not have a tag on it (small length of webbing or rope for you to grab). I always use a 4 metre lead rein with a clip end (rather than a loop) when teaching a foal to lead, and these can be used as a figure of eight rope if you need one later[5]. In my box of equipment, I also have a piece of ribbon about 3 cms wide and 2 metres long, a scarf, a freezer bag clip, a couple of shoe laces and a small towel (for wet foals).

With the right set up, foals need not be kept in and isolated while they complete their training; there is great value in them being kept in a stable herd environment where they can learn from other calm horses. This will also take the pressure off you to get the job done and allow them to stay on a natural diet.

---

[4]*The best headcollar I have ever owned and the one featured in most of the photographs was made by Plas Equestrian, Plas-y-Mista, Rhy-dargaeau, Camarthenshire. SA32 7JJ. www.plasequestrian.co.uk. Plas Equestrian and I have now developed the 'Wild Pony Headcollar' which has a buckle available on both sides of the head and both ends of the noseband.*

[5]*My favourite lead reins are also made by Plas Equestrian as above.*

Your facilities need not be posh but they do need to be safe. Given sensible fencing and careful manoeuvring the foals should be able to go back with their mothers or friends between training sessions and be turned out in the field. If you are going to work with unhandled foals on a regular basis, it's worth erecting decent fencing which funnels them towards the stable or pen so that it's easy to bring them in and work with them. You are more likely to commit yourself to training your foal and more likely to succeed if you set yourself up correctly in the first place.

It goes without saying that semi-feral foals are unlikely to have met electric fencing before and are very likely to jump over or through it if you rely on it to fence them in. Accordingly I never use electric fencing either to funnel foals into a pen or as a temporary pen. The risk of injury is far too great and, if they do get free, that is something else negative that they have learned. I am also wary of gates and hurdles where the foals are just tall enough to think about clambering over them and may get a leg caught on the way. Post and rail is probably the safest if high enough. Do I need to say that barbed wire fencing is very dangerous?

For the pen, post and rail is fine providing the rails are neither too close together nor too far apart—the foal shouldn't be able to get its leg caught nor should it be able to get through the gaps or even think that it might be able to. Make sure there are no nails sticking out or anything else that the foal could get caught up on especially when he has his headcollar on.

Patent round pen mesh panels are ideal because they are tall and have a gap at the bottom where the handler should be able to roll out if there is an emergency. However, do be aware that very small ponies can get their feet caught through the squares if they roll and even smaller ones might be prepared to try the roll

Proper round pen panels with a roll-out area at the bottom.

27

out facility! It's unwise to leave a pony with a headcollar on inside a mesh panel pen as it is possible for buckles to get caught in the corners of the mesh squares. Builders' panels should not be used for pens as the wire is easily bent and could trap a small foot. The ideal shape for a pen is square as this encourages the foal to find a "comfortable corner" where he prefers to stand when you work with him; for this reason, I avoid round pens for this type of training.

If you are working outdoors you need to be mindful of wet weather and avoid setting up in an area which is going to become slippery. Never be tempted to work on a hard surface—if the foal did decide to rear and he fell over backwards it could be fatal.

It is always helpful to work in a stable especially as it is under cover, but make sure that there is nothing sticking out that could hurt you or the foal, so hay racks, salt lick holders and even mangers will have to come out. Unless you have full height walls, make sure that all partitions are safe and unbreachable and pay particular attention to the door. You need to be able to get out if there is an emergency, but make sure that the foal isn't tempted to jump over the bottom door. A full grill rather than anti-weaving grill might be useful, or you might just need to make the door temporarily higher. If you use mesh as in my story above, beware that the foal may not see it, and for the same reason make sure that any windows, especially if made of glass, are covered safely.

A 4 metre by 4 metre stable or pen is probably big enough to work in with most native pony foals, but you might want a bigger area for a bigger foal. You need to reach a compromise between being able to get out of the way and not trapped if the foal does circle or panic, but small enough so that he can't avoid you really easily.

The idea is not to put so much pressure on the foal that he feels like leaving, but the above precautions will make it easier for you to relax in your work and make it far less likely that you or your foal could be injured. What you are aiming for is a quiet, reliable environment where you can work peacefully with your foal.

To this end, you might want to park a quiet pony or the foal's mother in the stable or pen next door with a bucket of water and a pile of hay to keep them happy, so that the foal has a further calming influence around him. He may well go and stand next to this pony while you work with him.

The kick test!

As a final safety note, once you start working with the foal, make sure you keep thinking about safety. Take care to keep out of the pony's kick zone and beware of being bitten. If you put too much pressure on some foals, they may attack. Whilst clicker training can be used to ask a pony to bring his head round to you, with big, aggressive or older ponies it may be necessary to get a rope or headcollar on before you start to touch them and you should think about getting expert help; many semi-feral ponies will be very frightened of ropes having encountered them before. Don't let your ego get in the way of asking for help if you need it. See "Chapter Eight: What to do if you get stuck" towards the end of this book.

MOVING YOUR FOAL TO THE PEN OR STABLE

If you have some preparation time, it may help you to bring your foal in to the place that you are going to work with him. Establish the stable or pen as a nice hotel. Regularly feeding him in there with a friend may mean that you can ask him to follow a bucket when you want him to come in. Failing that, your foal can be gently driven in perhaps behind a friendly pony. Anyone working with you to bring the foal in must be calm and sensible and use minimal body language to put gentle pressure on the pony to persuade him to come in. Walking towards him with arms outstretched and people at regular intervals will usually encourage him to go the right way—make sure that no-one is blocking his progress and gate holders can help by having their eyes down and turning their body away. Think about where it is you want him to go and make sure that your body and intent is focussed in that direction. Once he starts to move, you can reward him by walking slowly and everyone putting their arms down. Think calm sheepdog. Shouting, running or chasing will cause him to panic and try to escape.

Low pressure driving.

Into a safe area.

If you have to separate your foal from another pony, try to do this by using quiet body language and resist the temptation to block him with gates and doors—a foal is inclined to keep going and then bang his pelvis on the door as he goes through.

Dunnock, Magnum and Rowan:
The Diary of the Three Musketeers

IN November, I was contacted by Audrey Scott-Hopkins about her three New Forest foals.

"I have recently purchased three New Forest foals and would love some advice on teaching them to accept human contact. Of the three, one came well handled and is not a problem, although if his friends tell him it's scary, he flies off with them, which is quite understandable. Foal two is coming round very nicely and will accept a good scratch provided I am either sitting down or on the far side of the gate. Foal three is the first to come to call, but he stops short of being touched and hides behind his friends, and will fly off at the slightest movement. Foals two and three were totally unhandled when they came here and were removed from their dams, driven over here in a cattle trailer and chucked into the field—not unusual I know but traumatic all the same. If I sit with them they will happily eat their supper when their bowls are very close to me, they will touch me, but foal three will not allow me to touch him. They are curious and seem happy, but I wonder if the four weeks that we have allowed them to settle in is long enough and whether it is time to start their "human" training?"

I arranged to run a "Handling the New Forest Foal" course at Audrey's later that month (and many of the photos in this book are of her foal, Rowan). Despite the fact that all three foals have the same sire, all three were extremely different in character. Magnum, who had been well handled from the start, came round very quickly and was happily accepting his headcollar in minutes. Dunnock was quite wary to begin with but within 10 minutes of using clicker training with him, he was asking me to put the headcollar on. Little Rowan, the shiest of the three, took the longest to accept the headcollar. When he was first touched with the hand on the stick he really kicked out but was happily accepting touch by hand within half an hour. I learned that he had been wormed in the trailer when he arrived and that it had been quite a struggle.

After day one of the course Audrey wrote:
"The boys were very happy back in their field, and Magnum had a good scratch as I fed him—no running off tonight. I am really looking forward to tomorrow." And, after day two: *"It was so exciting to see the foals come out of themselves."*

Two days later, she wrote:
"I have had the boys in for a couple of hours and in that time Magnum has been leading round the yard—no issues. Dunnock had his headcollar on with a couple of clicks, lead rope, no problems, and ended up being led up to the garden, round the drive and back. He met Granny through the window, watched the farrier working on Victor and calmly walked back down to his friends. Big click, a little more work and back in with Magnum. Rowan has begun to find the clicker a bit of a game, and will cross the stable to come and touch me/halter. I got him as far as willingly choosing to put his nose in the noseband hole about 20 times, and left it there. He did whip his head round once and flick the whole halter out of my hand and gave himself an awful fright, but he had a little sulk in the corner while I leant on the door and ignored him and then came back over to "play" again. I left it on a good note."

The next day:
"Magnum, no pre-amble, head collar on and led around the big yard by a very proud "father". Michael was well impressed at his progress.
Dunnock (kiss-me-now-cos-I-love-you)—no preamble, head collar on and walked around the yard like an old pro—very proud Dad as he chose him!! Rowan—he happily plays the halter game provided he can stretch his neck and not get too close."

And the next:
"I definitely made progress with little Rowan today. I did the stick, duster, hand bit for a while and got a little further up his neck. Then I went and leant on the stable wall by the door to see whether he wanted to work. He came straight over and did touch/click/treat for a while, followed by nose in the hole, click/treat. By the time we stopped he had the head collar noseband all the way up his nose, click and treat while he still had the band up his nose. He seemed to be really into it, but we stopped at that as the light was fading.
The other boys had 10 minutes each of halter on/off and leading".

"Magnum learned the difference between walk and trot on his lead rope. He really took to it like a duck to water. We did stand, legs, lead, walk, trot and finished with picking up feet – clever boy! Oh, and he met Granny through the window too! Dunnock, halter on/off = good fun. Up and down the drive 4 or 5 times, but not got the hang of what trot is, but walked/turned really nicely. Put his rope round one of the gate bars and got him to stand still while I did legs and feet. He only pulled back the once and as I was on the other end of the long line as you suggested, he ran back safely a few feet and then I gently reeled him in again. He stood like a lamb while I did all 4 legs and picked up his feet several times".

A week after the course, I went back to do more work with Rowan and spent time desensitising his face with a ribbon before putting a headcollar on him.

Two days later:
"What a difference. I fiddled about for a bit to help him to relax, he was very wet again, so a bit of time with the towel, and then I played with the bit of ribbon. He progressed very rapidly to the ribbon halter and lots of face rubs. I then started with the open halter up the neck with lots of face scratches. I did 10 repeats, and then I decided to see how he felt about the headcollar going straight up his face closed. I worked on standing at his right and getting him to have semi cuddles as part of his reward. He now likes to lean heavily into my side with my arm over the top of his neck scratching the opposite side of his face. He likes kisses on his face and at the base of both ears. Once he really got into that and was so relaxed that I was having to lean forward to reach him, I then was able to take the head part over his neck, pass myself the buckle underneath his chin and then put my arm clean round the front of his face, partially obliterating his left eye and knocking into his left ear whilst I fumbled to do the buckle up. "

"Sian was really amazed at the progress that they had all made. She hasn't seen them for a week, but she thought that the change in Rowan was truly astounding!"

Two weeks after the course:
"Just to let you know that the three boys met the farrier today. He was so sweet with them. Magnum and Dunnock met him in the yard in a most business like fashion. Halter and lead rope on, big strokes, sniffs of farrier apron, legs stroked, front and back legs picked up. He then tapped their hoof with the trimming tool, and Dunnock even allowed him to pick his foot out with it. Good boy! We went into the stable to meet Rowan. He had a lead line on for the first time. Guy just stroked him all over, let him sniff him and his apron and ran his hands halfway down his legs. We left it at that as he had been a good boy and we did not want to fluster him. A very successful visit overall. He was actually here to do the minis."

Later the same week:
"I was fiddling about with Magnum today and introduced him to the measuring stick. He was totally unfazed by it. Rowan was a good boy and allowed my 6 foot 7 inch son to stroke and scratch him."

CHAPTER SIX
The Technique

A detailed explanation of the "touch and move away" psychological technique to training your foal from first touch through to putting the headcollar on; tips for overcoming his fear and making things easier for both of you including the use of clicker training.

IT IS much more logical and ethical to train a foal to accept touch first before asking him to accept a headcollar. Desensitising him and then asking him to accept a headcollar in a non-confrontational way produces dramatic results in a non dramatic way. Forcing a headcollar on to a semi-feral or untouched foal trapped in a crush or restrained by humans can do irreparable damage to your relationship with him. Neither is it logical to say that this teaches a foal to have the headcollar on, to be led, to accept touch or to be caught. It simply forces him to do so.

The technique described uses gentle mental pressure and release to teach the foal what we want and that he can trust us. The headcollar itself is never used

Friend or foe?

to restrain and it is only when the foal starts to be led that he is introduced to physical pressure and release and asked to stay with us and move with us. Although the foal is asked to cope with pressure, it is the release that teaches; I use the phrase "reward" to describe that moment of release although technically it is not a reward it is the cessation of a negative stimulus. However, semantics are not particularly helpful when training foals and "reward" describes the spirit in which the release is given.

Before going into the pen or stable, it's a good idea to think about how you can lower your own adrenalin and energy levels, bearing in mind that the foal will look to you to see how he should feel. If you can be calm and reassuring in touch and word, that will help him to be calm too. Avoid highly caffeinated drinks or sugary food before you go in—they will affect your heart rate and energy levels; I know from experience. Also have a think about who is around you and avoid sceptics until you are really confident of what you are doing. Deep breathing and false (or even genuine) yawning will encourage your foal to do the same and to start to accept you as a leader and a partner rather than the predator that he most fears. Whilst unhandled ponies can be challenging, the challenge is actually with ourselves; can we slow down and control our body language so that we don't represent a threat to an essentially wild creature?

It's most unlikely that horses understand the words we use, but they do recognize a kind intent and if we use words that reflect that, in a calm way, then they feel less threatened. A low pitched voice with lots of long vowels is much better than a high pitched, quick voice. If you have a tendency to go up an octave or two and to speak more quickly when you are nervous then it's probably better not to speak at all. I always think that "ssshhh, ssshhh!" and "Steady! Steady!" are Equus for panic. Whilst you need to be in the moment and to read your foal's body language, you can also afford to think about other pleasant things, so that you aren't becoming too focussed.

Be prepared to work with what you have got and beware of taking it personally if your foal doesn't want to be with you at first or takes a little longer to come round; just accept that your foal is doing what he thinks he needs to do in order to survive.

With the hand on the stick, the feather duster and your own hand you need to be firm and not tickly when you come into contact with the foal's body. A flat, rhythmical, violin bow action soothes more than scratching or patting. An unhandled foal will not cope with being patted at all. I suggest to people that they use the sort of touch they would give their best boyfriend, girlfriend or teddy bear if they were massaging them.

If you work in a calm and quiet way, with low adrenalin levels, then there is no reason why the sessions with the foal cannot take place over a few hours.

Nevertheless, it helps if you can stop at suitable intervals, preferably on a good note, to allow the foal to rest properly, to have a drink and something to eat and even to rejoin his friends. When you start again, you need to re-cover some of the steps you have introduced before so that you can consolidate what you have done and make sure that the foal isn't pushed too far, too fast. A good horseman is one that takes a lot of steps on the way to his ultimate goal but the best horseman is the one that creates even smaller steps and is prepared to go back over them. If you focus too hard on the ultimate goal, you become the predator that you have been trying to avoid. You may want to split the work up into several sessions over a few days and it does help if you can work on consecutive days to begin with. However, you will be surprised by how much tamer your foal is the next time you go to him. Good technique followed by his own latent learning often means that foals make amazing progress in a very short time indeed.

Now that's what I call wild!

Finally, be aware that touching a foal for the first time can be a very emotional experience. I always feel that it is a great honour when an essentially wild animal allows us to touch him. The speed with which they learn can be awe inspiring and the co-operation they offer humbling.

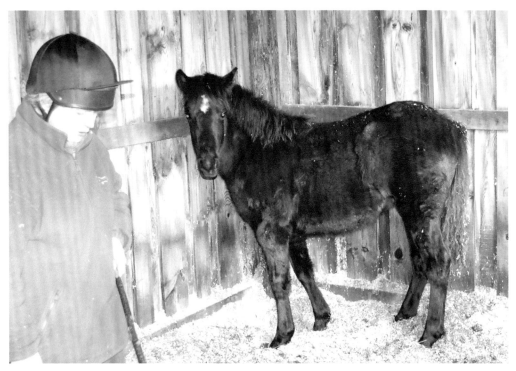

Taking the pressure off.

THE TOUCH

ENTERING THE PEN

When you enter the pen for the first time, you need to stay by the door and gently turn away from him so that you can see him in your peripheral vision but you are not giving him direct eye contact. Direct eye contact is very significant to horses, especially unhandled ones and is a mental pressure upon them. The easiest way to take that pressure off is to turn your eyes away or down. Depending on how wild the foal is and what kind of treatment he has received before, he may run around the pen a little. Providing you are not in danger, try to just stand still and just be. How he reacts will allow you to gauge the situation and will give you a lot of information. You will see which side he prefers to place you—it can be either the left or the right and you may see where he prefers to stand—his "comfortable corner". Let him relax and get used to the fact that you are there and that you mean him no harm. Quietly observe his body language at this stage—you might spot a slightly tightened under-jaw, high neck carriage or what could be interpreted as a resting hind foot. Just be aware that this is far more likely to be a running foot—just like an athlete on the starting blocks—he is reserving his right to flee.

CHOOSING A SIDE

The fact that your foal offers to you one side or the other is incredibly significant. It is very rare for a semi-feral or nervous foal to allow you in to both sides of his body. Most will either let you in to the left or in to the right—some will only let you look at their bottoms! I have heard all sorts of theories to explain this phenomenon—for example, that horses, like humans are either right handed or left handed (or should that be footed?) and have a natural preference to use that side first; the other which I really like but is equally unproven is that foals tend to travel on one preferred side of their mother when they are afraid. The outside eye in that case would be the "guard eye" and therefore the side that they are most likely to offer to you; the inside eye would be the "soft eye" which they keep close to their mother – indeed I am told that this is the eye that they keep close to the udder of the mare when feeding, leaving the guard eye on guard. Having observed New Forest herds at length, I am not sure of the veracity of this and my foals have fed from both sides of their mothers. The significance though is that this will influence which side you work with the foal to begin with. This will also be the side from which you will put the headcollar on the foal. You might not be able to work with the other side at all until the headcollar is on.

Because all of horsemanship comes from the military, through the Pony Club and British Horse Society, we tend to do everything from the left hand side of our horses. In the army it didn't matter whether a soldier was right handed or left handed, he had to be right handed in battle and his sword was fastened to his left leg so that it could be drawn by his right hand. It was imperative that his horse was on his right hand side or he could injure it with his sword as he drew it. How many foals have really struggled with having their first headcollar because we insist on doing everything from the left? It doesn't make sense to them.

THE COMFORTABLE CORNER

The comfortable corner is also useful as by very gently driving the foal back in to that corner if he moves around, you can bring his adrenalin down and help him to relax.

TOUCH AND MOVE AWAY TECHNIQUE—THE FIRST TOUCH WITH THE HAND ON A STICK AND THE FEATHER DUSTER

Offering the hand on a stick.

Now you can start to work towards the first touch with the hand on the stick. Slowly extend the hand towards the foal's nose—about 1 metre away and if he so much as looks at it, take it away to reward him—you can also drop your eyes and move your body away from him. This pressure on, pressure off will form the pattern for all the work that you do. Approach with the false hand again and see if he is prepared to reach out towards it. If he does, take it away immediately in order to reward him. The idea is not to leave it in place for him to get used to it but to show him that if he is prepared to allow something close to him or to touch him, you are prepared to take it away again. This allows him to relax and bring his adrenalin down again. The message is "I am not a predator" and it is critical to realise that it is not the touch that teaches, it is the move away; the release. Continue in this way to see whether he is prepared to touch the hand on the stick with his nose. If he does, take it away immediately to reward him and then repeat it three times. You'll see that he becomes braver each time he touches it because he knows that it will go away. He may even press into it.

If the foal cannot cope with facing the hand on a stick or begin to think about touching it, then you needn't insist and can just go on to the next step. Next, gently point the hand on a stick sideways on towards his shoulder keeping about a metre away. **If he threatens to kick at this stage make sure that you are still by the door and that you are well out of his kick zone. If he comes backwards towards you then you need to accept that you may have a real kicker and either think about clicker training (see below) or refer to the chapter at the back.** If he stands still, take the hand on a stick away immediately to reward him for standing still – you can also drop your eyes and move your body away from him. If he moves try to keep the hand on a stick with him but at the same distance until he stops moving and then take it away to reward him. Try not to react by exclaiming or rushing and remember to breathe. The message is that if he stands still, the hand on a stick will go away but that if he moves it will stay with him but it will not hurt him or chase him. Once he accepts this, you can go closer with the hand on the stick and repeat this technique until he is relaxed about that. You can touch him for the first time and, if he stands still, even if he flickers his skin, take the hand on the stick away and again, think about dropping your eyes and moving or turning your body away. Repeat this over and over again until he no longer flickers his skin. After the first couple of touches, you might in fact leave the hand on the stick on his skin until he stops twitching and then move it away to reward him for coping with the hand on the stick.

Touch and move away technique.

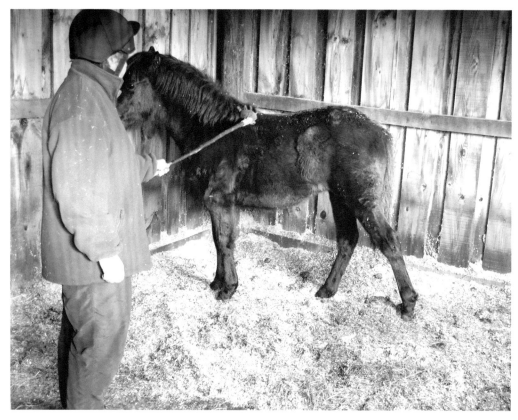

Base camp at the withers.

Once the foal is comfortable with the initial touch you can begin to rub him at his withers—just a few rubs at a time—with the hand on the stick. This is where the firm but rhythmical violining or "doing-the-ironing" motion helps. It is forwards and backwards across his withers rather than side to side along his back. Rubbing him in this position will remind him of when his mother rubbed him at the withers to bond with him and to encourage him to drink when he was first born. Remember to take the hand on a stick away from time to time and to lower your eyes and move or turn your body away. You can now move from the withers along his back using the same rhythmical technique. Quite often the pony begins to enjoy this quite quickly but it is still important to go away from time to time to prevent his adrenalin levels reaching a peak. If the foal does move away at any time, just try to quietly keep the hand on a stick with him or close to him until he stops and then reward him by taking it away instantly—you could also lower your eyes and move or turn your body away.

Some foals cannot cope with an initial touch here and as an alternative I may touch their bottom instead. Taking great care not to get kicked, I would proceed in exactly the same way but high up on their rump and having established a first touch here then work along their back to their withers. If a pony does kick out, it is possible to teach them not to do it by keeping the hand on a stick in place until they stop kicking and then taking it away to reward them. Simply, this shows them that kicking out won't work but I would urge great caution in this situation. It is very easy to teach them that kicking does work.

Once you have established that you can rub between their withers and their bottom, in whichever direction, you can start to introduce some subtlety. By observing the foal's body language, you can wait until he shows some sign of softening—for example, a blink of the eye, lowering of the head, turning his head towards you, licking and chewing, breathing out or putting a running foot down—and choose that moment to take the hand on a stick away. Even if you aren't able to do this, it's still important to move away from time to time and sometimes it helps to count in order to do this—rubbing for a count of five at first, increasing to ten, fifteen and then maybe twenty.

Base camp at the bottom.

A soft expression.

Desensitising the neck.

Having rubbed all along the back from his withers to his bottom, it's possible now to move outwards from here. It is best not to go to vulnerable areas such as the tummy or the legs at this stage but you can start to work your way up his neck, over his neck and to his chest. By rubbing outwards from the withers, you move rhythmically to a new area and go just a little further before moving back again to the familiar areas. The art is to head back just before he might object.

Once the foal is accepting touch with the hand on the stick albeit only on one side of his body, I would then switch to the feather duster. Once again, this should be offered to his nose first and then you proceed in exactly the same way, covering exactly the same steps—just as slowly. If he objects or threatens to kick or bite, you may have to go back a step and re-establish touch with the hand on the stick. If you stop the session for a break, it is prudent to begin again with the hand on the stick rather than assuming that he will automatically be fine with the feather duster.

Touch.

And move away.

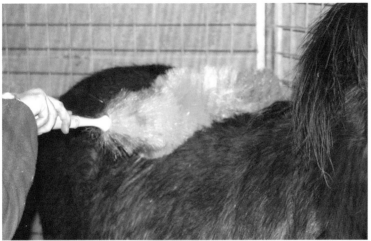

Violining motion across the back.

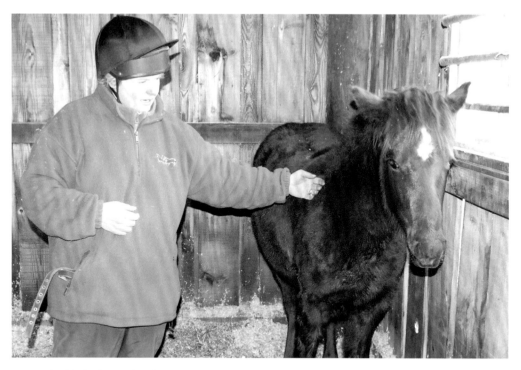

Using the back of your hand. It may help to face the rear as well.

THE FIRST TOUCH WITH YOUR OWN HAND

The next step is to touch him with your own hand. At first, just reach out with your arm about a metre from his shoulder and if he stands still, take it away again instantly to reward him – you can also take your eyes away and move or turn your body away. Repeat this at least three times and until he can cope with it. If he moves at any stage try to gently go with him and put your arm down the instant he stops. Next you can touch him at the withers and then move your hand away to reward him. Most foals hardly notice the change from the feather duster but those that have encountered predatorial behaviour from humans before, where the hands may have been close to their head, are more likely to object. To make yourself less like a predator, you can use the back of your hand first and make sure that you are standing facing the foal's rear end with his head in your peripheral vision. Once you have established first touch and repeated it at least three times, you can turn your hand over and start to rub him at the withers. Be gentle, don't scratch and don't tickle. Try to feel the tension of his skin pushing back at your fingers and to use a massage type touch—you want it to be the best touch he has ever felt. You then use your hand just like the hand on the stick or the feather duster repeating every single step in exactly the same way—just as slowly. In time, the foal will accept your body a lot closer to him and may even lean in to you.

The next step is to put two hands on him working in unison and rubbing in exactly the same way. From here you can make sure that he is happy for you to have a hand on each side of his neck and to have your body much closer to his.

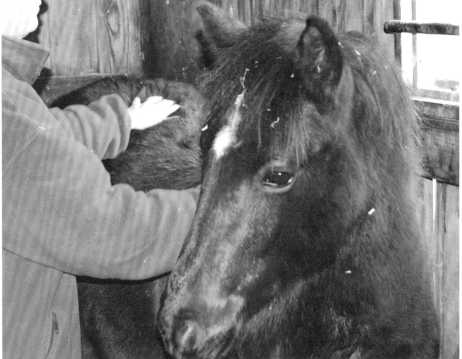

One hand and then two hands—a piano!

It's worth spending a lot of time at this stage getting him used to you being right next to him with your side against his. You can touch and move away with your hip in exactly the same way as you have before until he is comfortable with you touching him quite firmly. You might even find he leans in to you and some foals certainly reach a turning point at this stage where they feel reassured by your proximity. Having worked your way all the way up his neck with your hands, you can then start to desensitise his face. Use a very soft touch here and work on tracing the bones of his cheeks and gently rubbing him between the ears and the eyes if you can. Some foals may object strongly to this but by slowly persevering you can usually touch their cheeks at least. It's at this stage that you will learn whether your foal is particularly ear shy on one side or both. Avoid touching the muzzle at this stage as it is very sensitive in all horses.

Throughout this process you may encounter the foal deliberately touching you when you approach the same place a few times especially on the face where he might offer you his cheek and press it into your hand. This is known as a "sweet spot".

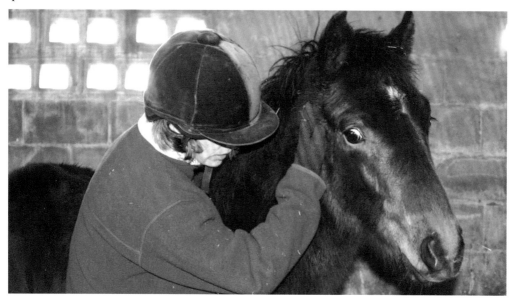

Desensitising his face with a kind hand.

DESENSITISING THE OPPOSITE SIDE

If at any stage your foal ends up with his opposite side facing you, you could take the opportunity to work with that side of his body. Go right back to the beginning and use the hand on a stick at first. If he allows you to work with this side of his body, you might find that he becomes much softer on this side and relaxes incredibly. Having let you in to what he feels is his most vulnerable side, he then learns that there is nothing to fear. However, if he turns the other way again, you needn't force the issue and can wait until he has his headcollar on or you get a further opportunity.

Throughout this time, you have been approaching and moving away from your foal, providing him with plenty of pictures for his photograph album. At first you'll see that he braces himself as he compares your approach to the pictures already in his album. In time, he will really relax and is more likely to open the album at a page where there is a good picture of a person approaching him. On the handling courses I run, a foal may be trained by two or more people, one after the other, so that he has pictures of more than one person approaching him in a nice way. The proper name for this process is systematic desensitisation.

THE HEADCOLLAR

You should now be able to touch the foal with the headcollar. However, you may wish to work with something like a ribbon or a soft scarf first. Ribbons and scarves are a wonderful thing for foals that are really struggling to accept a headcollar perhaps through having met one before. The ribbon or scarf can be used to touch and move away and then draped over his back. Any initial concern soon diminishes as the foal realises that it isn't going to hurt him and then you can play with it over his body and around his face and gently close it around his nose. Foals seem to really enjoy the sensation and lack of resistance in fabric used like this.

Once you feel that you are ready to move on to the headcollar, make sure that the crown piece and the noseband are both undone. Rolling it up in your hand with the buckles carefully placed at the top where they can't touch the pony, use exactly the same technique as you have used with the hand on the stick, feather duster and your hands—and just as slowly. The idea is to show him that nothing changes in your technique.

Using a scarf to desensitise the face.

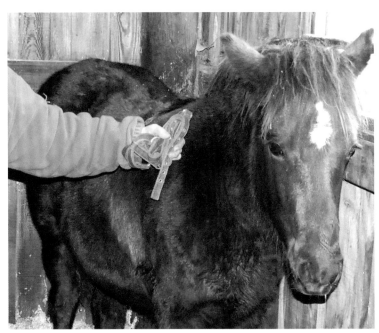

Rubbing with the headcollar.

Once he has accepted being touched in all the same places with the headcollar, you can lay it on his back. Putting the headcollar on from behind like this, is much less threatening than trying to slip a noseband over his nose straight away. The nose is the most sensitive place on the foal's body and he will instinctively react to anything enclosing it. This, coupled with two predatorial hands in front of his face is likely to make him flee. When placing the headcollar on his back, if you remember that the long strap goes on *his* left back, no matter which side you

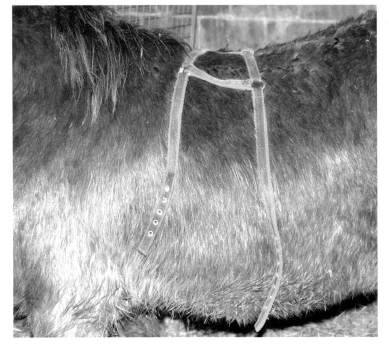

Long strap, left back.

are on, you cannot go wrong. Long strap, left back. With the headcollar laid out in this way, just go back to rubbing him with your hands and leave it there for now. If you think about the rubbing rather than the headcollar it takes your focus away from it and makes you less predatorial. If he moves away, the headcollar which is balanced on his back shouldn't fall off and you can gently go with him until he stops without having to hold on to the headcollar. You can then reward him when he comes to a halt by taking your eyes away and moving or turning your body away. Go back to rubbing him as if nothing has happened.

Next, you can move the headcollar 5 cms forward up his neck and go back to rubbing as if nothing has happened. Continue to move it 5 cms forward and then to give him a lovely rub until the headcollar is halfway up his neck. Whichever side you are on, you should then be able to reach around his neck very quietly and bring the back straps together and do them up. If he moves away, you shouldn't attempt to restrain him with the headcollar as he will go into pressure and panic. Just stay with him quietly until he stops, reward him by moving away and then carry on.

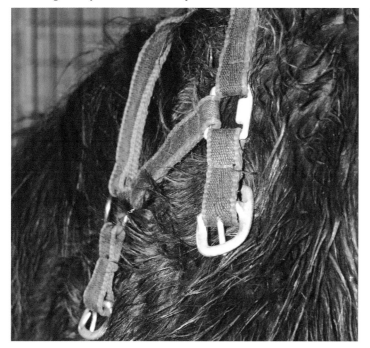

Inching up the neck.

Once the back straps (crown piece) are done up, move right away from him to give him the biggest reward that you can. When you approach him again rub him first and then make sure that the headcollar is turned the right way up—this may mean gently pulling it round his neck for half a turn. Once it is the right way up, carry on rubbing for a little while and then move the crown piece 5 cms up his neck. Resume rubbing and repeat this until the crown piece is behind his ears. It is worth moving away again now while he gets used to the noseband which will be loose next to his face. When you approach again, resume rubbing him.

Taking the pressure off once the crown piece is done up.

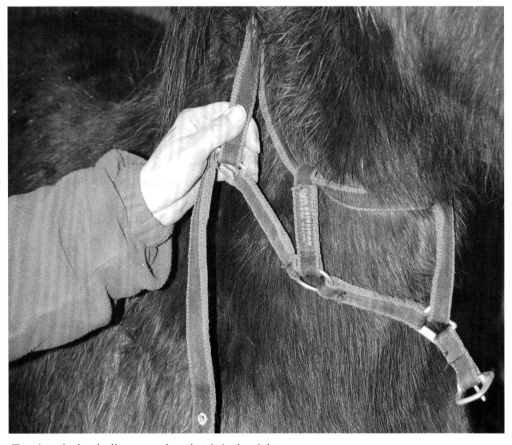

Turning the headcollar around so that it is the right way up.

The next step is to desensitise him to the noseband. With your arms on both sides of his neck whichever side you are standing, take hold of the buckle with your left hand and the very end of the strap with your right. Then just touch his nose with the strap and move it away, repeat this three times or more until you are satisfied that he is coping with it and then gently thread it over his nose and do the buckle up. It may be necessary to do the buckle up with one hand—a skill that is worth practising. Once again, avoid restraining the foal at any time with the headcollar as he will go into pressure and struggle.

Final steps before doing his headcollar up. Note this pony was happier with me on his right.

TAKING THE HEADCOLLAR OFF AGAIN

As a general rule, I would take the headcollar off again and then repeat this process twice more before ending that particular session. I take the headcollar off in the normal way so that the pony starts to feel the noseband move down his nose. Unless the foal is particularly quiet, it is best to leave lead rein training for another session. I am very wary of leaving anything but a breakable leather head collar on a foal so I usually take the head collar off again and start again the following day. Foals can easily hang themselves or be badly injured when a headcollar is left on.

There is a huge message in taking the headcollar off —remember it is the release that teaches—and I think they are always happier if they think they are not going to be confined forever.

If the headcollar gets left on, it is too tempting to not bother practising the technique. Too often I am called out to foals that have regressed through lack of attention and commitment and they cannot be caught again. In the meantime their heads have grown and their headcollar hasn't and they are in danger of being injured or starved.

PUTTING IT BACK ON AGAIN

The next time you go to work with your foal start right from the beginning again but it is normally possible to proceed very quickly indeed to the headcollar stage. Once the foal is really relaxed about having the headcollar on you can start to put it on in the traditional way, sliding the noseband up the nose done up. Some foals prefer you to be at the side to do this—rather than flipping the crown piece over the head, it helps if you can just put your arm over the foal's neck and draw the crown piece across. Others would rather you were face on.

In a short time you should be able to start putting the headcollar on your foal in a larger and larger space. It helps if you can expand the space incrementally, perhaps starting in the yard and then a small paddock. The approach is exactly the same —use some touch and move away with your arm and hand before working with the headcollar and if necessary go back a few stages if you need to—either by going back into a pen or putting the headcollar on in the original way.

No fear, no force.

SPECIAL EFFECTS

Whilst the basic technique works very well for the majority of foals, I have found that there are some little ruses that can help where you or the foal get stuck at some point.

For example for foals that are really frightened of hands, I have found that by taking a little of the waxy residue off the teats of a mare (even if it isn't his own mother) and rubbing it onto my hands I can get their interest quite easily.

If you are working outdoors and the foal is wet, he isn't going to appreciate it when you rub him and let the water past the oily protection of his coat to his skin. An old small towel can be really useful here as you can wrap it around the hand on a stick, or if you are further down the line, your own hand, and rub him with it to dry him off. The towel soon smells of him and seems to give a lot of comfort. Equally it can be wrapped gently around the neck or placed over his back as further desensitisation.

On an odd occasion I have had a foal learn that he can dislodge the headcollar from his neck by shaking himself; a plastic freezer bag clip can be invaluable here as you can just attach the headcollar to his mane each time you move it.

Shoelaces provide an excellent extension to the straps of your headcollar. Tie a knot in one end and thread it through an eyelet. Where a foal is struggling to accept the noseband perhaps because it brings you too close, you can pass the noseband and lace over his ears and gently down his face and then thread the end of the lace through the buckle and gently draw the two ends together. You can then pause before quietly doing the buckle up.

Taking the shoelace out again once the headcollar is on.

Occasionally a foal will learn that circling while you are working will postpone you; it's his job to avoid hassle in his life and, as it isn't a good idea to get trapped in corners with him, he can soon learn that this delays things. Once I suspect that there is a pattern of behaviour, I will often use a second passive person to just come into the pen and act as a "blocker". When the pony turns his head to circle away from me, that person can look him in the eye and gently raise their palms towards him. This usually has the effect of mentally blocking his escape and just asking him to engage with the main handler. There is no question of that person being used to restrain the pony or getting big in any way. It's very gentle "good cop, bad cop". In the same way, a pony that presents his bottom like a pendulum to dissuade you from working with him can be gently discouraged by the presence of a second person in a different position—he can only point his bottom at one person at a time.

CLICKER TRAINING

For foals that are accustomed to eating hard food, I have found that clicker training in order to put the headcollar on is a really fast track method. It is great to see a foal positively asking for his headcollar to go on in order to get his click and treat.

Clicker training involves the marking of a behaviour with a noise, usually a click and then rewarding the foal with a food treat. If you do use clicker training to train your foal to have his headcollar on, this doesn't mean that you have to use clicker training for everything else you ever teach him to do although I would say it is a very powerful tool to have in your training repertoire especially in emergencies. I think there would be value in every horse having at least some clicker training for this very reason even if it isn't used very often.

Some schools of horsemanship warn against the use of food as a reward as it can give them a very odd message. Horses determine their position in the herd hierarchy by moving each other around and taking one another's food. The leader of the herd is the one that can move all of the others around at will and move them off their food. When we give horses food we could be giving up our place in the herd hierarchy.

If you are going to use clicker training you must be very disciplined about the way you use it if you are not going to encourage your foal to become pushy or nibbly; Monty Roberts, for whom I have a great deal of respect, is adamant that horses should not be taught to associate the human body with food. However, by adhering to strict guidelines, such as never rewarding your foal for touching you and never giving him hand treats without him hearing a click, I would hope to avoid these potential problems. I would justify my use of clicker training by pointing to the massive progress that some foals make when offered clicker rewards. Clicker trained foals tend to progress more quickly than those that are not trained this way, to start to come up to be caught and to want to follow you on a lead rein. Sometimes it's almost as if there has been a click in their psyche too and they become very imaginative and more willing to try. Badly executed clicker training can however produce some nightmare ponies that are inclined to invade your space and nudge people for food.

I have no doubt that some clicker training purists could also frown on my cherry picking approach to training methods around foals especially as I am inclined to combine clicker with other methods such as pressure and release. I am between the devil and the deep blue sea. My technique could also be condemned because I fail to use a proper clicker, I just make a "tlock" noise with my mouth—you need to practise this—and I do use it to reward demeanour as well as tasks. Accordingly, I may give a click and a treat to a pony when I hear him breathe out deeply, lower his head or soften in some way. There is nothing complicated about clicker training if you think of the click as being the equivalent of a "thank-you" for behaviour that you want to see—to me, it is the same as moving away or lowering my eyes as a release of mental pressure. No doubt, if you were going to use clicker training as your main method for training, you would need to tighten up on some of the ground rules but that shouldn't prevent it being used casually but carefully for training unhandled foals. I would call it Positive Association Training instead but as you know, I don't believe in PATting!

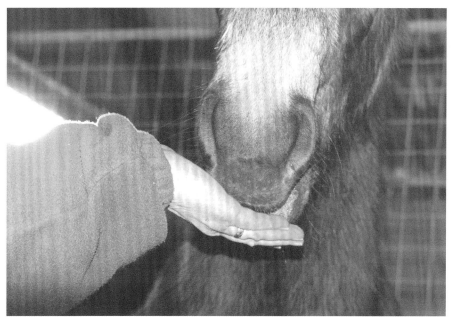

. . . and treat.

Sadly, clicker training cannot be used with every unhandled foal as some will refuse to take unfamiliar food from the hands of a predator. Cheap and cheerful food such as simple pony nuts is often more palatable to semi-feral foals that are very suspicious of expensive mixes. Where a foal is happily taking food from a bucket, it doesn't usually take them long to accept it from the hand providing they have not had a headcollar forced on them previously.

HOW TO USE CLICKER TRAINING

It is important not to skip the touch and move away process as it is more ethical to put a headcollar on a foal that is happy to be touched than one that is not. But, if you have a foal that is inclined to kick then clicker training is a great way to encourage him to bring his front end round to you and may save you having to put a rope around his neck or having to restrain him in some way. However, if your foal becomes over excited or aggressive when you start to clicker train him, think carefully about whether to proceed and if in doubt, refer to the "What to do if you get stuck page" at the end of this book. Some semi-feral foals and indeed some domesticated ones have learned to mug for treats and can become aggressive when offered food.

Having gone through the whole process of touch and move away with the hand on the stick, feather duster and your own hand if safe to do so, you can then start to clicker train the foal. At this stage the feather duster is going to come in handy again but you should be aware that it's significance changes at this stage and it becomes a tool in your clicker training kit and should always be used in conjunction with clicker treats from then on if you are not going to confuse your foal.

First, point the feather duster at the foal's nose and if he touches it, make a "tlock" noise with your tongue and then give him a treat. One or two pony nuts at a time is plenty and you need to think about reducing his every day rations by the amount that you have used in your clicker training. The treats can be stored in your pocket or, even better, a brightly coloured bum-bag so that he eventually associates that bag with his clicker training rather than just you. The "tlock" needs to be given the instant he touches the feather duster target but you have about three seconds to give him the treat. He should be asked to take it nicely rather than grabbing at it. Offer the feather duster again and when he touches it repeat the click and treat and then continue to do so until it is clear that he associates touching the feather duster with the audible click and then the treat. He is likely to experiment to see whether anything else produces a click and treat so he may try to search your body to see if that will make a noise. You can just be passive providing he doesn't get pushy and wait until he touches the feather duster again before giving the click and treat. If he does start to nudge or nibble, you can use a little body language such as "chicken wing" arms and a "kiss-kiss" noise to send him away from you a little. Try not to use physical contact as this is likely to activate his "into pressure" response and he will become more physical with you.

Once you think he has made the association between the target (the feather duster) and the click and treat you can test this by moving around a little way to see if he will follow the feather duster or stretch for it. Next, put the rolled up headcollar with noseband done up, in your hand and ask him to touch that instead. If he does, he gets a click and a treat. You can repeat this a few times before holding the headcollar up unfurled and asking him to touch that for a click and a treat.

Next you are going to change the rules and ask him to allow you to touch his nose or cheek with the headcollar and when he does, again he gets a click and a treat. He may be surprised, confused or even upset that you have changed the rules. Foals join a union very quickly and like the rules to stay the same. Repeat the touch several times for a click and a treat and you can start to hold the headcollar on his face for a few seconds longer each time before rewarding with the click and treat.

Next, very quietly put the noseband over his nose a little way and take it off again and give a click and a treat. If he goes backwards try to stay with him a little until he pauses and then take the noseband off and give a click and treat. Repeat this step a number of times until you are able to put the noseband over his nose for a few seconds before giving the click and treat. After this, try leaving the noseband on his nose holding it gently with one hand and give a click and

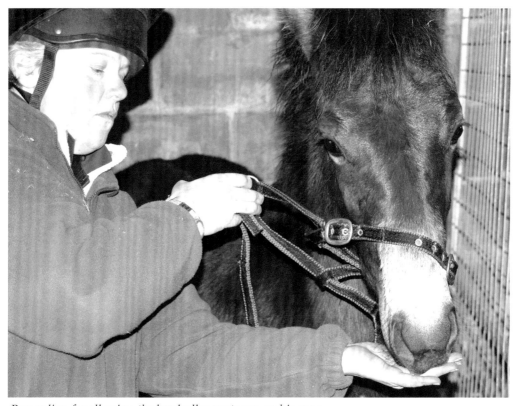

Rewarding for allowing the headcollar part way up his nose.

a treat from the other hand. Once he is settled with this, you can take the crown piece and touch him on his right cheek in return for a click and a treat. Once he is happy to have the crown piece held against his right cheek, you can gently push the end of it across the top of his poll and then give him a click and a treat. The final step is to fasten the buckle of the crown piece and give him a click and a treat. Here, I might be tempted to give him what is known as a bonus, a small handful of pony nuts this time.

Logically, the next step is to take the headcollar off again and I am in the habit of giving the foal a click and treat once the headcollar is off as this encourages them to stay with me. I would then repeat the whole process a number of times until the foal is really quite relaxed about having the headcollar on. This whole process can take less than 15 minutes and don't be surprised if the foal gets a little avid and stands there willing you to put the headcollar on.

The next step is to start cutting out some of the stages and treats and it isn't unusual to be able to put the whole headcollar on in one go (and then click and treat) within the first session of clicker training. Nevertheless, it is easy to go back a stage and to introduce more stages and more rewards if the foal gets a little worried—beware however that he might start to train you and remember that click and treats are wages not bribery.

FRIENDLIER FOALS

The touch and move away technique and clicker training may still be useful where a foal appears to be friendly. Where foals are happy to be touched they may still be disinclined to allow you to put a headcollar on them easily. Quite often they have been able to pick and choose when they want to have contact with people, to engage and to disengage at will, and they can sometimes object to being asked to stay in one place or to having something put around their face.

FOALS THAT ALREADY HAVE A HEADCOLLAR ON

I would still want to establish touch first even if a foal arrived with its headcollar on especially if it appeared that putting his headcollar on was the full extent of his official halter breaking. There is a lot of difference between halter breaking and halter training and it bears repeating that it is often easier to work with unhandled foals than manhandled foals. Where foals have had a headcollar forced on them before, they can be extremely worried about having hands anywhere near their face. It can be an advantage if the foal already has his headcollar on as you may be able to clip the lead rein onto the headcollar and influence his movement and in particular keep his back legs away from you. It can also be a huge disadvantage if it has been done badly as he may be extremely wary of having another headcollar on. Providing the headcollar isn't compromising his welfare, you can start of with some leading rein training as described in the next chapter before revisiting the issue of the headcollar. Once he has learned to give to pressure then you can gently hold him with the lead rein whilst putting another headcollar over the one he has on. By repeatedly putting a second headcollar on and then taking it off, you can desensitise him to the headcollar without having him loose. The easiest way to lower his adrenalin and yours is to set out to put the headcollar on and take it off one hundred times but then stop when it is clear that he's okay—this is usually at about thirty in fact! Once again, if the foal is accustomed to taking hard feed, you can introduce clicker training to promote a positive relationship with the headcollar.

Dartmoor Pony Training Centre
The Story of Alfie

THE Dartmoor Pony Training Centre was set up in 2005 initially to take on ponies either left unsold at the markets, those going for low prices to dealers or those donated to them for one reason or another . Later the work expanded to encompass more promotional work for the breed. Founders Natalie Torr and Kathryn Hulland attend many of the local sales and offer people information on how these amenable ponies can be brought round using ethical methods. Dartmoor ponies often prove to be excellent family ponies once they have learned to trust people. The ponies and foals in the care of the Dartmoor Pony Training Centre live in a herd environment and are introduced to hard feed very early on so that they are amenable to clicker training. This proved to be a great advantage when Kathryn was working with Alfie. This pony had been required to face his trainer at all times during his initial training using a rope around his neck to pull him round. This requirement, which is commonly used with older horses trained in so-called "natural horsemanship", is often too much for a frightened and vulnerable foal and isn't necessary—they will usually start to look at you voluntarily in their own good time. As a result of being pulled in this way, Alfie couldn't cope with any pressure on his head at all and would rear instantly if he was pulled.

"I slowly built up a trust with Alfie and used clicker training to teach him to be caught and groomed. He seemed to love it. Eventually, I taught him to back up, move over and even to pick up his feet. You could see he was concerned to start with but he took a leap of faith because he knew he'd get a treat!" says Kathryn.

Since 2007 I have been working with the Dartmoor Pony Training Centre demonstrating the techniques I use. As well as proving to die hard commoners that the techniques I use are still effective, I needed to prove to Natalie and Kathryn that they were not too demanding of the foals. Happily I was able to satisfy them and they have felt able to support me in the writing of this book.

The Story of Autumn

I WENT to meet Autumn in September, 2007. This pretty forest-bred New Forest yearling had quite a character. Even though she was only in an ordinary wide webbing headcollar, she was very difficult to lead. When her owner applied even the smallest pressure on the headcollar, Autumn would plant herself on the spot, her eyes would droop and she would drop to the floor. Observing her closely it was possible to see her lean into the headcollar searching out the endorphins that would send her to sleep. The owner told me that the behaviour had started the instant the pony had been tied up and seemed to be a well rehearsed pattern. Following my advice, Tina asked a Chartered Veterinary Physiotherapist to have a good look at her and the physio found that her poll area was very tight and sore. In the meantime, Tina used a quarter rope around her pony's hindquarters to prompt her to move her back legs first rather than activating her into-pressure response at the head.

CHAPTER SEVEN
Lead-rein technique—teaching your pony to stop and go.

Covering how to introduce the first lead rein and how to ask your foal to follow a pressure and what to do if he says no.

AS explained before, horses are naturally "into pressure" creatures so that when you pull them their instinct is to pull back. If you stand close to them and push them then they will give you a push back. Whilst we can teach them that we want them to follow a pressure or move away from a pressure, until they have learned that or whenever their adrenalin is high, their first instinct will always be to go into pressure. Young foals may not want to be with a human, which they may see as a predator, and won't lead automatically. The first time you pull their natural tendency will be to leave.

By using very gentle pressure and release on the lead rein, we can start to ask them to follow a pressure but this is an incremental process. Having said that, it rarely takes very long. Once taught, it doesn't mean that they will never go into pressure again and we still need to take special care to make it easy for them to do the right thing.

Put your gloves on before starting lead rein work. Once more in an enclosed environment, you can gently clip on the lead rein as soon as your foal is relaxed about having his headcollar on. It makes sense to touch and move away with the lead rein at the shoulder before clipping on. The ideal length for a lead rein is about four metres as this means that you don't have to be very close to the foal, you have time to react if he tries to run away and yet you are not going to get caught up in long lengths of rope.

Keeping your body language low and standing off to one side, the first step is to apply a gentle pressure on the headcollar until your foal moves an ear towards you. The instant he does so, release the line so that there is slack in it—a so called "smile in the line". Have your hand palm down on the lead rein so that you can apply a steady but slightly elastic pressure rather than a jerky on/off type pressure. You could repeat this a couple of times before asking the foal to turn his whole head towards you. The instant he does so, he gets the release back in the line and in this way learns that he has done the right thing. Once again, repeat this a few times before asking him to move a front foot towards you, remembering to keep at an angle to him. Avoid looking him straight in the eye as this will discourage him from moving towards you—look at his feet instead. In this way you can perfect your timing so that the instant he moves towards you, you can take the pressure off to reward him. It doesn't matter if he moves back to where he was. At this stage we are not interested in straight lines, just teaching him the concept of pressure and release. You should find that in no time at all he becomes really light in the hand.

Move at an angle to him.

If at any time he tries to leave, you can apply a steady but elastic pressure and gently go with him until he stops and then reward him by putting the smile back in the line—try not to actively restrain him and try not to speak—a "steady, steady, steady" at this stage will have the opposite effect. In this way he learns to come to a halt and that you will reward him for that by going away. The restraint needs to be really gentle and passive. I think of the pressure and release as being like Jim Trott in The Vicar of Dibley—"no, no, no, no, yes!"

If your foal hasn't been desensitised on his other side by this time, this is a good point at which to begin working on it. You can try gently holding the foal in place while just looking at his other side and then moving back to his favourite side to reward him. Once he accepts you standing on the other side, you can begin the touch and move away technique going right back to the hand on the stick to be on the safe side. As I mentioned in the last chapter, you may find that once he has allowed you into his other side, he becomes really soft in his attitude.

From now on, you should be able to ask your foal to turn in either direction towards you but you shouldn't expect him to come right up to you at first. Leading can be taught in relatively few short sessions taking care always to end on a good note.

Once he understands the concept of following a pressure you can start to work in a larger area and ask him to take more steps in one go before giving him a release in the line. Avoid becoming too ambitious and make sure you are working in a safe place with good fencing and a soft surface. At some stage he is likely to go into pressure and pull away from you. It's helpful if you don't over-react, allow him a little more line, apply a steady elastic pressure and keep low to avoid him rearing and flipping over. It doesn't matter if he needs the whole of the line. Think of yourself as an elasticated post rather than a solid object. At this age, the foal is particularly vulnerable around the poll and it is best to avoid strong pressure. Go back to a smaller area if there is any risk of him getting away from you, and consider walking out with another horse when you first start to go in straight lines.

Leading outside for the first time. The flooring here is made of rubber.

From a risk point of view, I was horrified recently to read a book where it was suggested that it was good practice to tie a foal to his mother's surcingle to teach him to lead. I can't imagine what would happen if the mare or the foal was to take fright and panic.

LEADING TECHNIQUE

This is one area where Intelligent Horsemanship practice is definitely different from the British Horse Society and if your foal is being prepared for showing it may conflict with what you will need to do in the ring. I believe that the position in which to lead a foal is with his head in line with my body rather than me being at his shoulder. In the herd, horses lead from two positions—in front (generally a mare) and driving from behind (stallions). By standing at the shoulder we are neither one thing nor the other and we are asking the foal to take the lead—a position he may find frightening. Neither do I like the foal to walk behind me. In this position he can switch off and should he then be startled he can run straight over me. Alternatively he could start to experiment with domination from behind, putting his ears back and taking up a driving position. With the horse at your side you can keep him in your peripheral vision and see what he's doing and keep up a constant dialogue between you. I also use the "motorbike hand", i.e. my hand palm downwards. Once his initial training is completed, when you are ready to walk then you just walk. Looking him in the eye will discourage him from coming forward. Once he is moving next to you, clearly establish a "smile in the line" so that there is no pressure on his head at all. When you want to stop, just stop and use an elastic pressure to ask him to stop too. Later you can introduce basic groundwork to teach him to stop without any pressure at all.

Leading practice.

RELUCTANT LEADERS.

If a foal proves particularly reluctant to lead or plants himself and refuses to go forward, it may be sufficient to just move at an angle to him and ask him to move again. If he continues to go into pressure you can avoid applying more pressure to his head and poll by employing a figure of eight or quarter rope around his hindquarters. This need not be a rope at all—a soft piece of fabric such as a scarf will work just as well and is very nice to use with very young foals. The foal needs to be comfortable with you being right next to his body by now and it is critical to desensitise the foal to the feel of the line or fabric around his bottom by using the touch and move away technique at first and then gently holding it in place. Once he accepts it, a gentle pressure can be applied to the quarter line just before or at the same time as using pressure on the head. This asks the hindquarters to move forward—at first he may rush a little but by keeping calm you can show him how it works.

As a matter of interest, I have taught a foal to lead by placing my jumper over his back and using the sleeves around his neck to ask him to move towards me. This wider more comfortable pressure took the focus off his head and poll and was less likely to activate his into pressure response. When I eventually decided to put a headcollar on him, he led very lightly from the outset.

Gentle pressure on the hind quarters.

An alternative method for reluctant leaders is to ask a second support person to slowly walk behind the foal slightly off to one side and about 3 metres behind. They need to remain passive and low in their body language until you ask them to help you. If the foal starts to drag or pull back, they can use very light body language—perhaps just patting their coat or lifting their hands up, to ask him to move forward and keep up. The instant the foal goes forward, they need to drop this body language and become passive again to reward him for doing the right thing. It is rare to find a foal that doesn't react to very slight body language but ultimately this support person could rattle a plastic bag behind the foal or a small plastic bottle with gravel in it.

Once you have taught your foal to accept touch, his headcollar and to be led, you should find that he no longer views you as a predator but sees you more as a leader and a partner.

What a Difference a Day Makes—The Story of Honey (By Amanda Strowbridge)

Amanda and Honey.

AT the end of the summer in 2008, I received an email from Sarah inviting me to attend a Wild Foal Handling day in the New Forest. I had recently returned to Dorset from living in London and had got back into horses after a break of almost 20 years. I was intrigued to say the least.

I had just been through one of the most difficult periods of my life and had nearly lost my home, business and everything that I had worked for. Suffice it to say I was not in the best emotional state of mind.

We met the filly, who had never been touched by human hand, and had been described as a "bit of a wild one" by her owner. After quietly herding her into a pen, with mum next door, Sarah showed me the various techniques to gradually gain the foal's trust. The foal was wary but also curious and after the use of various methods such as the hand on a stick and feather duster, the foal allowed us to slip the headcollar on with complete trust and no force. Once she had her headcollar on and off three times we opened the pen to allow her to leave. She was in no hurry and happily stayed with us for another ten minutes just investigating our clothes and being stroked.

This was one of the most rewarding experiences I have ever had. There is something profoundly moving when a wild animal, whose every instinct is to flee, trusts you enough to let you touch it all over and then fasten something onto to it's head. The whole thing took less than ninety minutes. I returned to see her two days later and after another lovely rub, I was able to put her headcollar on almost immediately.

The foal in question was for sale and inevitably, I bought her. I called her Honey and she was delivered a couple of weeks later when she had been weaned. She has proved to be the most loving trusting pony I have ever met. I am so lucky to have had an immense bond with her from the outset.

Incidentally, I have since worked with three more wild foals on behalf of friends and the same technique, learned in just one day, has worked for each of them too.

CHAPTER EIGHT

Catching, tying up, ear shyness, foot handling and worming techniques

Explaining how to take an incremental approach to train your foal to accept these key tasks.

CATCHING

YOUR foal is only an extension of the initial handling technique. By approaching in a non-predatorial way, not looking him directly in the eye, and not going in a straight line, you are much more likely to be able to get close to him. When your foal picks his head up to look at you for the first time, reward him by turning or even walking away a little. Acknowledge this as his first offer to be caught. You can now continue to approach being careful not to look him the eye. If he walks towards you, acknowledge him in the same way. If he simply stands still then approach his shoulder on his favourite side and put your arm out towards him. If he stands still take it way again to reward him and do this another couple of times. Next, you can ask him to touch your hand with his nose by stretching it

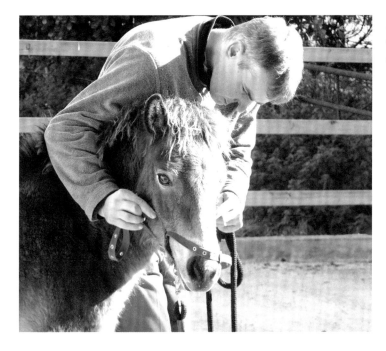

Nothing has changed, catching in a bigger area.

out towards him and respond in the same way by taking your hand away when he has touched it. Now see whether he will let you touch his shoulder and again, touch and move away perhaps three times. Depending on how confident he is, you can then put the headcollar on from the back if necessary—the message is that nothing has changed. If you have been using clicker training, then continue to use clicker training—you can give a click when he picks his head up the first time, a click if he walks towards you and a click and a treat when he stands next to you before clicking and treating him for having his headcollar on.

If he walks away at any time, just gently walk with him without rushing or exclaiming in any way and keep with him, at the same distance, until he comes to a halt. Move away from him straight away to thank him for stopping. This is more likely to draw him in to you and once again proves that you are not a predator. You may have to repeat this a few times and it helps if you can at least act is if you have all the time in the world. If you are in a hurry, you will become too focussed and predatorial. If in doubt, go back to gently driving him into your enclosed area or ask him to follow another horse or a bucket.

A lovely feed in the stable or pen is a good incentive for a foal to start asking to be caught. At the Exmoor Pony Centre we used to run a fishing game where the students would take it in turns to "fish" for a pony within a large group. Using the same technique they would aim to catch a pony within a group of about twenty. Once caught the foal would receive a feed just outside the training area. Within days the foals would be queuing up to be caught.

TYING UP

It's essential that your foal understands that he must follow a pressure before you tie him up for the first time and he needs to be very comfortable about being touched; otherwise he is likely to go into pressure very easily and to panic. Accordingly touching and leading are best established first.

The easiest approach is to pass the long lead rein through a ring on the wall with you still holding the end of it. If possible, you would also place panels or another safe barrier a little distance behind the foal to prevent him from backing up very far. At some stage, the foal will discover the tension in the line and his likely reaction, despite his earlier training, is to go into pressure. Rather than fight him, it helps if you can allow him to go backwards retaining only the gentlest elastic pressure in the rope until he comes to a natural halt. Then just ask him to come forward again using gentle pressure on the rope and when he is where you want him to be, give a release in the line. In this way he won't feel so vulnerable when he is tied up in the future and is less likely to cause an injury in the poll area at the time. Foals trained in this way are less likely to learn that they can pull back and break whatever they are tied to.

Pass the rope through the ring without tying it.

Only when this is well established would you actually tie your foal up and even then it is worth investing in a patent tie up bungee so that there is still some elasticity when he is tied up. If you must use baling twine to tie your foal up, then make sure that it is partially shredded so that it will actually break if he panics—I have seen a horse move an entire round pen when going into pressure against baler twine tied to the pen; it doesn't break easily. Foals should only be left tied up for a very limited period of time.

When your foal is tied up, try to work with him sympathetically. Untie him and have him in hand if you are going to do something he could object to. It is easier to apply pressure and release and to move him around if you are in control. If you leave him tied up, he may resort to blocking you with his bottom or self-defence if he feels vulnerable.

It is common for horses to scrape the floor when they are tied up—this is interpreted as a sign that they would like to be able to move. If you go back to your foal every time he does this, he'll learn that it gets your attention. Either ignore it or distract him by scraping your own foot.

EAR SHYNESS

Some foals are naturally ear shy; others become ear shy as a result of sensitivity to flies, having their ears twisted as a form of restraint or because they have had their ear tagged or cut for identification.

The best way to get over ear shyness is to give the foal some control over the training. Start off by placing your hand on the foal's neck as far up as you can go without the shyness being activated and then begin the touch and move away technique you have used before. Once your hand is immediately behind the foal's ear, wait until he moves his ear back towards your hand and reward him by taking your hand away. In time the foal will start to bring his ear back to actually touch your hand—continue to reward him by taking your hand away. In time you can wait until he has pressed your hand more firmly. From here you can usually choose to gently touch his ear and then move your hand away if he keeps still. If he does move, gently keep your hand with the ear and wait for him to stop moving his head and then reward him by taking it away immediately. Even if he moves his head vigorously it is usually possible to stay with his ear in a very passive way. In time you should be able to touch the whole of his ear and gently massage it. Foals really seem to like it if you carefully cup the ear at the base and rotate it in both directions.

Let him bring his ear back to your hand.

It is important that your foal is never grabbed and restrained by the ear and that any fly lotions are applied very gently and preferably at body temperature. By asking the foal to bring his ear back to "lick" the lotion off a hand you can get good coverage around the rim of the ear and it will eventually seep into the ear.

FOOT HANDLING

It is very worthwhile to teach your foal to have his legs and feet handled well before the first visit from the farrier. All too often foals are ill prepared for their first meeting with the farrier and through lack of time, or lack of empathy, the farrier may rely on strength rather than persuasion. The foot is picked up very suddenly causing the foal to become unbalanced and then held up very high for quite a long time. It's worth reminding ourselves that horses are prey animals and it is not surprising that they find this very frightening.

Once again it is important that he should have learned to follow a pressure and be comfortable with you being close to him before you begin handling his legs. It is much easier to work with him in an enclosed space as before and to have him in hand rather than tied up.

The first step is to teach the foal to keep his feet down while you handle his legs all over. Once again, you can use the touch and move away technique described earlier. It is not unusual for a foal, particularly a colt, to try to bite you, to strike out, to rear or to kneel down the first time you touch his legs. This is entirely natural behaviour that he would employ and practise with other colts. It's sensible to return to the hand on the stick for this initial handling so that you can avoid his teeth and feet if he deploys them and so that you can stay with the leg until he stops the behaviour. Starting at the shoulder for the front legs and the rump for the back legs, you can start to touch him down his legs. If he moves or

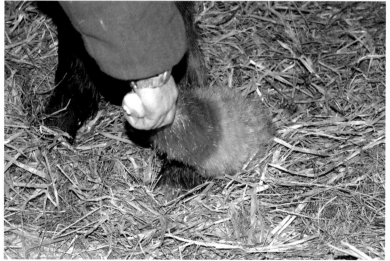

Rubbing the fetlock.

reacts then just stay with the leg but move the hand on a stick away to reward him the instant he is calm. In this way he will learn that *this* is the behaviour that you want.

Once he is quietly standing with his feet down while you touch them with the hand on the stick you can switch to the feather duster and repeat the training again. When he is relaxed about the feather duster you can start to use your hand instead. You may well find that he is very happy to be gently scratched between the fetlock and the hoof.

Once he accepts that you can touch his legs, the next step is to give him a clear cue that you would like him to pick up his foot. You can do this by gently squeezing the tendon in the lower leg or the chestnuts. Pulling at his foot or his feathers is counter productive because it will unbalance him—in physics we were taught that every action has an equal and opposite reaction. When he picks his foot up the first few times, there's no need to hold it at all. You want him to just learn that this signal means "pick your foot up". Once he understands this, to teach him to keep his foot up, you can gently cup his hoof and support it at the front with just two fingers. Because he is bearing all of his own weight, it will be far less frightening for him to maintain this stance and it will be much lighter for you to support. Hold it up for just a few seconds at first and not very high. In time you can hold his foot higher and for longer and start to pick out his feet.

If he lifts his foot up, stay with him until he puts it down.

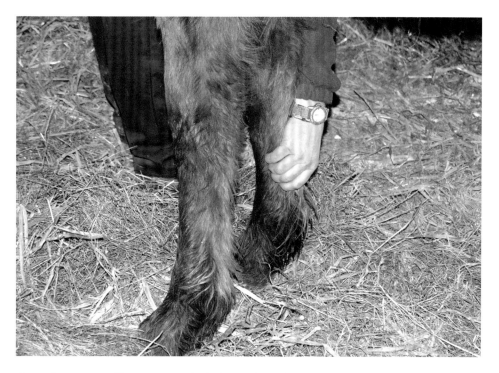

A gentle squeeze will encourage the foal to pick his foot up.

Holding the toe very lightly to encourage the foal to balance himself.

Worms expelled by an Exmoor foal even before he was wormed.

WORMING

All foals and especially semi-feral foals can have a very high worm burden even at a young age. It is a myth that free-roaming ponies self medicate for worms and foals are susceptible to worms through grazing soiled land, through their mother's milk or even in utero. Even before you worm, you might find that your foal starts to expel a lot of worms as soon as he is on higher quality grazing. It is always advisable to check with your vet as to what type of wormer will be best for a foal and the correct dosage. If he will take hard feed or even just a forage based food, you can mix the worming paste in with it. One worming manufacturer produces worming tablets for ponies and some will eat these straight from the hand or mixed in with less exotic tasting foods such as pony nuts. I have resorted to making wormer paste sandwiches for one horse that was particularly difficult to worm!

There is absolutely no need to force a wormer into a foal's mouth using a worming syringe. Once the foal is tame, you can use the touch and move away technique with the worming syringe against his face to show him that it is nothing to be afraid of. Then it is simply a matter of inserting it gently into the side of his mouth and depressing the plunger. Foals rarely react badly to this or the taste

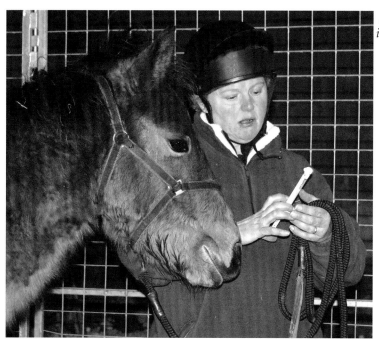

It's important to read the instructions.

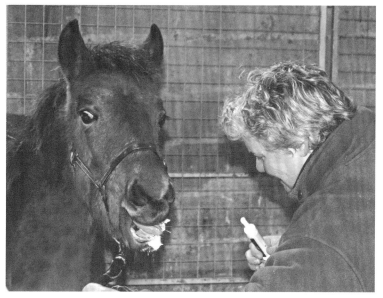

Whoops—missed!

once you have taken the time to desensitise them to the syringe itself. You can even create a happy association with the worming syringe by "worming" them regularly with sweet apple sauce.

Lateral or what I call "sideways" thinking is critical to good horsemanship. Finding a way to make it easy for the foal to do the right thing makes their lives so much easier and means that they can get rewarded for even the smallest progress.

The story of Billy Milton

Billy makes friends with Rocky in the snow.

BILLY MILTON appeared on Johnny Kingdom's Programme *A Year on Exmoor*.

David and I were house-sitting in Exmoor in the middle of a bleak February. Val Sherwin, the Chief Executive of the Moorland Mousie Trust had asked me to work with Billy just to make sure I was doing something useful. Only days before we got there, she announced that the BBC was coming to film me working with him.

On the first day of filming at the Exmoor Pony Centre, I used the techniques described in this book to touch him and to put his headcollar on. It took just less than an hour and Johnny was suitably impressed. Billy was then loaded to travel across to West Hollowcombe so that I could work with him when I had time over the next few days. By day four Billy was happily leading around the yard in the falling snow, walking over tarpaulin and making friends with a rocking horse. By the time Johnny came back on Day Nine he was very confident indeed. He walked straight up to Johnny and the camera crew and started to chew Johnny's hat, feather and all. He also washed some of the salt off Johnny's car!

When Amanda and Michael, the owners of the house returned from holiday, they were greeted by a camera crew and a sound boom. They didn't seem to mind and decided that Billy could stay with them and their other two foster ponies, Merrion and Robby. Later Billy was diagnosed with a respiratory problem and was therefore integrated into a conservation herd in Northumberland.

CHAPTER NINE
The confident foal

Explaining how to instil basic ground rules in your foal's life from the outset through very basic groundwork and clear body language and how to discourage unwanted behaviour.

Dunnock whispers in Michael's ear.

The amazing, amusing and disconcerting thing about training foals is just how quickly they can evolve from being wary and worried, to being utterly confident. Although they may still have moments of doubt, within no time at all they are testing the boundaries, trying out new behaviours and treating you as one of the herd.

Cello and friend, playing colt games out on the Forest.

Every aspect of a foal's behaviour *is* absolutely natural. Within the herd they receive some guidance from other herd members as to what is acceptable and not acceptable to other horses, but they have no inbuilt sense of what is and isn't acceptable to humans. Even within the herd they get away with things that would never be tolerated from older herd members. Within days of being born they run in front of their mother to block her so that they can have a drink, they clamber all over her head and chew her ears and later they help themselves to her feed.

Cello chewing his mother's ear.

This behaviour works for them, helps them to survive and teaches them about life. It's illogical and unreasonable to expect a foal to automatically know how he should act when he is with people. It is entirely unfair to punish a foal for behaviours including biting, kicking, pawing, striking out, rearing, bucking and fleeing, all of which are an important part of their repertoire. It is also quite ridiculous to expect them to understand English although they can learn to understand a verbal cue from its tone. We need not tolerate these behaviours. The art is to find a non-violent way to show the foal that this behaviour is not acceptable to us.

Sadly many horses do not meet with very clear rules when they are with humans. They may be allowed to nudge their handler whenever they like until the day the handler is at a show and wearing a clean white shirt. Then they might be smacked for nudging. Apart from the confusion this may cause, there is a deeper problem here. Horses determine their place in the herd hierarchy by moving each other around—the leader is the one that can move all the other horses around. When a horse can move its handler around, subconsciously it may assume that it must be the leader. For many horses being herd leader is an extremely responsible and vulnerable position to be in. For foals it could be terrifying.

Ideally you will begin to establish some basic ground rules as soon as your foal arrives, even when there is still a blurred line between the foal being timid or brave. By using subtle but sufficient body language you can establish your leadership very quickly and discourage behaviour that you don't like without ever having to use violence. This will set your foal up for life. It is instinctive for him to test you from time to time just as he would check his position within the herd hierarchy, especially if he remains entire.

There is absolutely no harm in being affectionate with your foal providing you avoid over-doing it. The affection should be on your terms rather than his, and be mindful that he may start to demand attention if he discovers that this behaviour works for him. Be wary of hand treating unless you have the discipline of clicker training—it is almost guaranteed to produce a nibbly foal; occasional hand feeding actually reinforces pushy behaviour even more.

There are two places on a foal that should not be over-handled—the muzzle and the bottom. Handling a foal's muzzle seems to activate their desire to nibble. If you watch two foals together they are always nibbling each other's faces in an attempt to dominate. If you scratch a foal's rump too often, you will find that he starts to walk backwards towards you inviting you to scratch. This may be misinterpreted by someone else and the foal may be unfairly punished. Also, this behaviour is not so funny when he's 14.2 hh and his rump has grown to the width of a dray horse.

It's important for the foal to be allowed to be a horse and he will thrive best in a herd environment where he can be disciplined by older horses and play with other youngsters. If he is isolated or you keep him occupied whenever you are with him, he will soon expect you to be the entertainment committee or may develop ways of entertaining himself which are actually harmful to him. You also need to take into account the age of your foal when working with him— all sessions should be short and sweet, there should certainly be no element of drilling and ideally you will want to simply incorporate these ground rules and way of working into your everyday contact with your foal. By the same token, long periods without any contact at all may allow your foal to regress to his wilder behaviour.

Foals need not have perfect manners but they should certainly have good enough manners. Your foal should never learn to move you around and you should be the one moving him around.

Orphaned foals may have missed out on important social lessons from their mothers and other herd members, and the sooner you can fulfil their social needs (as well as their nutritional needs) the better. To avoid them becoming totally humanised and being out of place with other horses, integrate them into a small group of placid horses as soon as you can.

BASIC GROUNDWORK FOR FOALS

As well as leading your foal, it is useful to train him to stand still, to move forwards, backwards and from side to side. These sessions can be really short and eventually you can just incorporate your ground rules into your everyday interaction with your foal. Before you start, have some idea of the rewards and body language that you are comfortable using. By now, your foal should appreciate a lovely rub as a reward for doing the right thing—either on the neck or on the forehead between the eyes. Your body language might be as subtle as tapping your coat which can be increased where necessary to slapping your coat, making chicken wings out of your arms, pushing your palms out towards the foal or even jumping up and down if necessary. There is a huge range of things that you can do in the scale between no rules and hitting. Any body language accompanied by a "kiss-kiss" noise can be used to good effect providing you have a clear intent behind you actions. If you make a request, follow it through so that the foal doesn't learn to ignore you, and be absolutely consistent. You may also need to rely on physical pressure and release from time to time.

Your foal will also tell you whether you have gauged the level correctly—if he looks as if he might like to leave the country when you tap your coat, then you need to be even quieter; if he doesn't budge an inch when you do it, you might need to get more assertive. If you can read your foal's body language and measure your response accordingly, that's when you become a true horseman. The great horseman Mark Rashid talks about halving the pressure when your instinct is to double it. As a general rule, I use very subtle body language when I am <u>asking</u>

Tapping the coat.

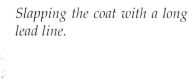

Slapping the coat with a long lead line.

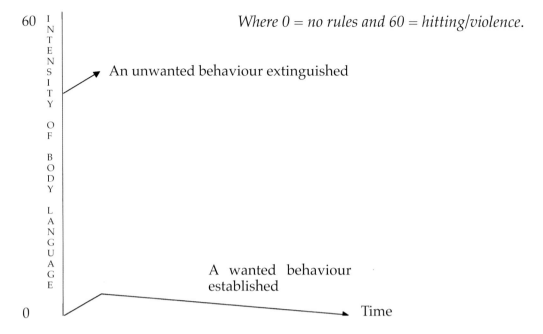

the foal to do something; and I might use fairly assertive body language when I am <u>telling</u> him to do something, especially when he has ignored my more subtle request a couple of times. I am more likely to use assertive body language for behaviour that I want to extinguish altogether.

ESTABLISHING YOUR BOUNDARIES—ASKING YOUR FOAL TO STAND STILL

It is instinctive to all horses to want to keep moving forwards. Accordingly a foal may find it quite hard to stand still even for a few moments. If you start by establishing your body space you can often get your foal's attention and bring down his adrenalin levels so that he is more inclined to relax and stand still. Position yourself directly in front of and facing him with about an arm's length to his nose and then ask him to maintain this distance. Facing the foal means turning everything towards him—your eyes, shoulders, hips, and feet. Keeping your hands down will prevent you from fussing with his face and stop you inviting him to touch you. Maintaining eye contact often helps to discourage him from coming forward but you should both be able to relax completely. There should be no pressure whatsoever on the lead rein. You can help your foal to relax by breathing deeply and yawning. You may see his head drop, his eyes half close, or a good lick and chew as he realises that he needn't worry because you are "there" for him.

If the foal moves forward into your body space then he should be promptly asked to step back out again. For some it will simply be a matter of taking a determined step towards them, for others you may need to make your body language very big—making "chicken wings" from your arms for example—or use a noise such as your rope slapping against your coat. Each and every time he steps into your space, it is important that you take that step back off him and one more besides. Be quite determined that it will happen; intent is everything.

This is the most important thing to establish with the foal and it forms the cornerstone of your future relationship. The foal learns that when you are around he can relax completely and let you take the leadership role.

MOVING FORWARDS AND BACKWARDS—THE STEP BY STEP APPROACH

By asking a foal to step forwards or backwards just one step at a time, he will learn to listen to what he is being asked to do and it will be easier to guide him through gates and into horseboxes and other enclosed spaces. One step is like one word and when you put individual words together you can form different phrases.

To ask for a step forward remain facing the foal but look at his feet rather than his face. In this way you are not discouraging him from moving forward and can also note when he has started to move so that you can be ready to ask him to stop. Take a decent step out of his space without putting any pressure on the lead rein and if he takes a step forward, block him so that he stops by using your arms as if you were conducting an orchestra. Give him a lovely rub for doing as he was asked. If he doesn't move forward then you can apply a gentle but persistent pressure on the lead rein until he does. When he comes forward use your block and then give him another lovely rub to reward him. If he refuses to move forward at all and goes into pressure, you can move at an angle to him and that will normally be enough to unplant him.

To ask the foal to step backwards you can also give a visual cue first—take one step towards his chest, no further than halfway along his neck and look at the foot that you want to move. Gently swing your rope against your coat three times and if he still doesn't move do the same again three times but more assertively. The rope should not come into contact with him at all. If he still doesn't move then you can apply pressure to the headcollar until he takes a step back. Once he has taken one step, give him a lovely rub as a reward. The foal should become lighter and softer in his response to your body language.

ASKING THE FOAL TO MOVE OVER

To move the hindquarters, start at the foal's head and move to his shoulder. Give him a lovely rub at the withers as his mother might have done, in order to establish a "neutral position". With a slack line walk along the length of his body before stepping out so that you are opposite his bottom and facing it with your eyes, shoulders, hips and feet. The more accurate your body language, the better the response you tend to get, and frequently the foal will step away immediately and bring his head round to you with no further pressure. In some cases you may need to tap your coat to get his attention. Once again he should get a lovely rub as a reward.

In time you can start to ask your foal to move away from a physical pressure just as you would ask a mature horse to move away from the leg when he is being ridden. Place your hand firmly on the part of his body that you want him to move and apply a little pressure. He is likely to go into pressure at first and push back towards you and he might even turn round to think about biting you—this is a natural response but by ignoring it, and being persistent and firm, he will start to think about whether there is something else he should be doing to release the pressure. The instant he moves that part of his body away, you should indeed release the pressure.

ANSWERING MORE DIFFICULT BEHAVIOUR

Biting is so important to foals—it tests and tastes new things and is part of mutual grooming, play, self-defence and later, courtship. Until they are shown otherwise, foals will bite humans without realising that it isn't acceptable—they may get confused as to whether we are their mother, their friend, their enemy or a potential mate. Once your foal is no longer timid you do need to make it absolutely clear by using assertive body language and a "kiss-kiss" noise that he is not allowed to bite you. Don't worry if he goes away and looks offended—he will come back. Providing you don't use violence it will not alter your relationship. Using body language in this way is preferable and more logical than using a physical contact on him which will actually encourage him to continue to engage in the biting behaviour. If you watch two foals playing together this is exactly what they do. Physical contact from one foal provokes physical contact from the other.

Biting can hurt and it's good to decide where your barriers are so that you can react the second your foal goes too far. For example, I am quite happy to allow a horse to touch (but not nudge) me with their nose, but I will react if I hear their mouth open. I am very adept at hearing that slight slap noise as their mouth opens. Slapping your coat and making a "kiss-kiss" noise until they back away a couple of paces is normally sufficient, however don't make the mistake of being wishy-washy; you must mean it. If you are vague at this stage, your foal may feel that it is worth trying to push the boundaries even more. Then his behaviour and the way in which you answer it will have to escalate.

I am also wary of allowing foals to chew equipment. It takes four years for the milk teeth to be completely replaced by adult teeth and during that time the foal must feel some discomfort. It is tempting to allow them to relieve it by chewing. The difficulty is that it won't be convenient or cute if they chew bits of expensive kit. Be consistent from the outset and insist that they don't chew everything within reach.

At some stage almost every foal will experiment with kicking out at you just as they have experimented within the herd. Often they have found that it makes others go away and they want to see whether it will get you to go away too. If this happens during the initial training process then you can keep the hand on a stick in place until the foal stops kicking. If it recommences at any time, perhaps because you are desensitising a more vulnerable area, you can always go back to using the hand on a stick. However, the easiest response when a foal kicks out at you is to clap your hands very hard and use a strong "kiss-kiss" noise to send him out of your space. In this way you can make it clear that this behaviour is not acceptable. The instant his head comes round and his bottom turns away, you can reward him by softening your body language and telling him what a good boy he is. If he kicks out and makes contact with you, it's generally because you have missed the warning signs —perhaps by putting too much pressure on him as you approach or by allowing him to "play" with you and to invade your space.

Pawing and striking out can usually be discouraged by doing it back without coming into contact with him. This usually distracts the foal very quickly and takes that bit of ground away from him. When a foal rears, a strong step in his direction, without getting in the way of his front feet, can have the same effect— avoid pulling on his head as he will go into pressure and could go over backwards.

With all behaviour it helps if you work out the reason underlying it—does your foal paw the ground because you are being too rough with a grooming brush or is he just expressing his desire to keep moving forwards by moving on the spot when he is tied up? If you are the cause of his behaviour then you can adjust your approach in the future. If you can see things from his point of view it can prevent him feeling the need to escalate the behaviour.

FURTHER EDUCATION

Your foal will enjoy going out for short walks as soon as it is safe to do so. Plan where you will go carefully and make sure that you have full control of him especially if you are going into public areas. You want the foal to develop a "follow you anywhere" attitude and to meet all kinds of new objects so that his comfort zone is steadily extended. This makes life so much easier when the foal is eventually ridden as a mature adult. In the home environment you can continue to desensitise him to as many novel objects as possible by using the touch and move away technique and allowing him to follow and investigate things. A slight word of caution—avoid letting him become a tourist; when he has had a good look at something, you should be the one to decide when it's time to move on. If your foal is frightened of something, it sometimes helps to back him up a few paces so that he can lower his own adrenalin and take stock. If you put too much pressure on him to go round or over things that he is afraid of, he may well learn to rush. Take your time and remember to keep your own adrenalin down and to breathe steadily.

Owning a foal can be an absolute delight as well as a huge responsibility. It can be daunting to have a blank canvas in front of you, but the foal is allowed to make mistakes and so are you. The more confident your foal becomes, the less worried he will be when things go wrong. You can consider any incident as a learning opportunity!

Orphan Annie's—The story of Freddie and Sterling

Freddie arrives at Orphan Annie's.

FREDDIE and Sterling were both orphans and it was appropriate that both of them stayed initially with my friend Ann whose stables then became known as Orphan Annie's .

Freddie's mother was run over when he was about 8 weeks old. He stood with her dead body all night until the agisters found him. Fortunately he started to drink his milk replacer straight from a bucket as no-one could get near him. He would turn his bottom on anyone going into the stable and threaten to kick them. I was asked to have a session with him and worked on touching him and eventually put a headcollar on him. From the first touch he was much happier about having people around him and a few days later he led beautifully along the lane and loaded straight into a trailer so that he could travel to Orphan Annie's.

Sterling was also orphaned at two months. Although he was brought in off the Forest and left in a large barn he had been given no supplemental feeding other than hay. By the time he was five months old he had the physique of a concertina file. I promptly bought him and took him over to Orphan Annie's for some intensive care.

By now, Ann was an expert on orphan foals. She had taken advice from both Jane Van Lennep at Simple Systems Ltd and Joanna Vardon at the National Foaling Bank who was somewhat flummoxed at the prospect of a foal that could not be held to drink from a bottle. Sterling was weaned back on to milk to which soaked grass nuts were added so that he appeared to be eating spinach soup. On this diet, both foals flourished. Sterling eventually went to live with Sheila, another friend of mine, and never looked back.

Both Ann and Sheila took great care to make sure that their foals were not over-handled and they were turned out with other ponies as soon as it was possible. In this way they didn't miss out on crucial early socialising.

Meeting these foals now, no-one would know what a precarious start they had in life.

Sterling—an amazing transformation from the two-dimensional pony that arrived.

CHAPTER TEN
What to do if you get stuck

THERE is a network of Recommended Associates of Intelligent Horsemanship throughout the United Kingdom, and most of them are prepared to travel a good distance to help people with their horses. All of them can be contacted via the Intelligent Horsemanship website at www.intelligenthorsemanship.co.uk where there is always an up to date list of the RAs and their specialities. All Recommended Associates have attended The Handling the Untouched Horse course that forms the foundation of the techniques described in this book.

Wherever possible, I am happy to answer enquiries by e-mail or telephone. I also run Handling the Semi-Feral Foal courses (and variations to that) as and when foals are available for me to work with.

FURTHER READING

There are a number of good books which I recommend to people who want to train their horses throughout their lives using ethical and logical methods.

Perfect Manners by Kelly Marks ISBN 978009 1882709 Ebury Press
Perfect Partners by Kelly Marks ISBN 0 0919 0087 5 Ebury Press
Perfect Confidence by Kelly Marks ISBN 978009 1917739 Ebury Press
—all available through www.intelligenthorsemanship.co.uk

Be With your Horse by Tom Widdicombe ISBN 0 7153 2020 3 David and Charles

Training Your Young Horse by Richard Maxwell ISBN 0 7153 2799 9 David and Charles

The 100% Horse by Michael Peace and Lesley Bayley ISBN 0 7153 2099 8 David and Charles

The Art and Science of Clicker Training for Horses by Ben Hart
    ISBN 978 0 285 6 382 4 2 Souvenir Press

Books about semi-feral ponies in Britain:
New Forest Drift by Sally Fear ISBN 0 9553253 0 7
Survival of the Fittest (A Natural History of the Exmoor Pony) by Sue Baker ISBN 0 86183 220 5
Ponies in the Wild by Elaine Gill ISBN 1 873580 11 8
New Forest Ponies by Dionis Macnair ISBN 1 873580 69 X

Appendix One

THE PRACTICE OF "SWINGING" OR "TYING ON"

I have sought the professional opinion of a veterinary surgeon and a McTimoney Corley Practitioner and this is what they had to say:

Over the last decade there have been huge advances within many aspects of veterinary medicine, and none more so than in the area of diagnostic imaging. Whilst most equine practices have had digital X-raying and advanced ultrasonography facilities for some time, an increasing number can now also boast gamma scintingraphy (bone scanning) and even CT and MRI. Our improved ability to pick up and diagnose a whole range of musculoskeletal issues means that we are becoming increasingly aware of the presence and significance of a whole range of neck and back problems, especially in relatively young animals, which may otherwise have gone undiagnosed. Whilst many of these 'injuries' can be attributed to a known traumatic incident, the cause of probably the majority often remains a mystery. For example, conditions, such as "kissing spines" and fractured dorsal spinous processes, are frequently first picked up in 5 or 6 year olds (whose increasing level of work finally uncovers an underlying problem); and we can often only assume that these injuries were acquired as youngsters through "messing about" out in the field, and from some other traumatic event, perhaps through human handling. And this is probably only the tip of the proverbial iceberg.

I have been a horse owner and rider for all my life, as well as an equine vet for over 25 years of them. I have also been a practising Commoner for the last fifteen years, with a number of breeding mares out on the New Forest. Whilst I have never actually witnessed the practice known as "swinging", all my instincts, both as a vet and as a horsewoman, tell me that it is not in the ponies' best interests, either physically or mentally. I have seen ponies pull back when tied up on many occasions (yes, vets can be frightening!) and have always been stunned by the massive force they can achieve, and the resultant damage to head collars, ropes and fencing. Whilst I acknowledge that it may a gross oversimplification to extrapolate this level of damage directly to the bony and soft tissue structures of the head and neck, I have absolutely no doubt that some level of physical injury, either temporary or permanent, will occur.

I have been honoured to have looked after some wonderful clients and animals throughout my career—and the ponies I see tend to be the ones owned by dedicated people who consider them invaluable. In contrast to this, the "cheap and cheerful semi feral pony" is often viewed as readily dispensable and of relatively low value and, as such, is unlikely to ever be presented to a vet. Hence, we rarely get to see these types of ponies at this stage of their lives, which makes it difficult for us to assess more accurately how such practices can, indeed, affect them.

Rebecca Hamilton-Fletcher, MRCVS

If, or should I say when, the foal panics it will pull back and all of the pressure from the narrow halter will be felt across the sensitive structures over and around his poll. As well as bruising to the superficial layers, there will be muscle damage and associated inflammation, which in turn will cause pressure on the nerves, resulting in what must be a very severe headache with associated heightening of light and sound; any migraine sufferers will empathise with this, it is not a pleasant feeling! Under the muscle at this point is the joint connecting the skull to the first or atlas vertebrae through which the spinal cord and nerves run. Pressure, especially pressure from pulling back, can cause damage to this important joint which is often referred to as the poll being "out". This may cause the nerves to be impinged resulting in pain and inflammation which could lead to behavioural responses such as becoming head-shy, nervous (especially when tacked-up), being difficult to catch, and having a high head carriage. It is important to remember that horses cannot verbalise their pain, so the only way they can let you know they are uncomfortable is through such behaviours.

In the foal, the structural disturbances described above would affect the growth and development of healthy tissue as the very young horse continues to grow. Any physical disruption to young growing tissue could have a negative effect on the horse physically, not just from performance and gait but may cause chronic discomfort. All this is just a physical viewpoint; I can't even begin to imagine the mental impact upon the young foal who has limited contact with humans.

**Kate Boe McTimoney Corley Practitioner
and Equine Sports Massage Therapist**

CREDITS

It would be wrong to write a book about horses without giving a great deal of credit to my horse Petra Perkins who was sent by the Horse God to teach me about quirky horses. When she completely trampled David and put my prospects of marriage in jeopardy I knew I had to find another way to communicate with my horse.

Lovely rubs too for all of the foals featured in this book which include Cello, Kanuthi, Harvey, Lilly, Dunnock, Rowan, Magnum, Billy Milton, Bryn, Honey, Freddie, Sterling, Foxtrot, Midas Touch, Trademark and Field Poppy.

Huge credit is also due to David (who is a saint), Kelly Marks who has been an absolute inspiration to me and to Carol Hartman, Ann Etchells, and Frances Moores for encouraging me to write. Carol also gave me the benefit of her professional expertise at no cost as she felt that the subject matter of this book was so important. Love to Julie Noviss and Sheila Reed who have always worked beside me and are blimmin' good at training foals. I have also been supported by Natalie Torr and Kathryn Hulland at the Dartmoor Pony Training Centre (www.dptc.org.uk).

Thanks finally to my Mum, Patricia, for brilliant editing particularly when I was writing at a gallop.

Photographs: Sarah Weston, David Vatcher, Ella Porter, Audrey Scott-Hopkins, Jenny Gilleland (www.jennygillelandphotography.co.uk), Natalie Torr, Jim Crouch.

All the best publishers have ponies. Carol and Gingernut.

THE BEST ENDING

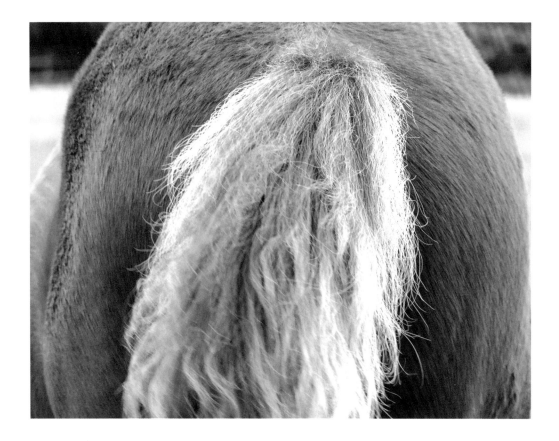